NO BOUNDARIES TOUR

The Fight Against Human Trafficking

Scott D. Gottschalk

SCOTT D. GOTTSCHALK

Copyright © 2025 Scott D. Gottschalk

All rights reserved. No part of this book may be reproduced, stored, or transmitted by any means—whether auditory, graphic, mechanical, or electronic—without written permission of both publisher and author, except in the case of brief excerpts used in critical articles and reviews. Unauthorized reproduction of any part of this work is illegal and is punishable by law.

CONTENTS

Understanding Human Trafficking...................................13
Prologue 17
Introduction 21

Chapter 1	Driven by Competitive Nature.....................	25
Chapter 2	Motorcycling Love Affair	35
Chapter 3	Death Wish on a Motorcycle.......................	51
Chapter 4	Grizzly Bears Not Biker-Friendly	73
Chapter 5	Motorcycle Devastation..............................	97
Chapter 6	Pushing Limits	129
Chapter 7	Years Planning World Record....................	145
Chapter 8	No Boundaries Tour Presentation.............	161
Chapter 9	Sponsorships and Press Release...............	173
Chapter 10	Pre-Ride Practice (We Can Do This!)	181
Chapter 11	Ride of a Lifetime Specifics	199
Chapter 12	Campaign Against Human Trafficking.....	201
Chapter 14	Motorcycling Quotes, Memes, and Laughter	211

We Only Regret the Rides We Didn't Take!

The authentic story of one man, one motorcycle, one country, one world-record charity ride to fight human trafficking for 120,000 miles, in 120 days, riding 18 hours a day, and 1,000 miles a day. HOW IS IT EVEN POSSIBLE AT THE AGE OF 70?

ALSO BY SCOTT D. GOTTSCHALK

The Folk and Their Fauna
The Story of One Man's Love Affair with Animals

The Folk and Their Fauna is a collection of true stories about domestic and wild animals. The author has taken some of the countless tales from his lifelong association with animals and written a sensitive book about those he knows and loves. His stories are sometimes funny, at times sad, and occasionally painful. Yet each incident shows an insight into the majestic cycle of living creatures. This book, with its eloquent descriptions of animal personalities, promises to entertain every animal lover. Indeed, like our attraction to animals, the appeal of this book is natural.

All the animals we cherish and love,
God made the folk and their fauna from high up above.
He bade we should share with each other united,
to keep a world that will remain undivided.
Man, and beast working side by side,
'Til the end of all time we shall always abide.
—Scott D. Gottschalk (1982)

Nine Lives to Eternity
A True Story of Repeatedly Cheating Death
An Inspirational and Faith-Driven Human Triumph

Nine Lives to Eternity is one man's true chronicle of cheating death a miraculous twenty-seven times. The author details the aftermath of his many harrowing experiences and mishaps, any of which should have resulted in certain death, yet somehow, he was incessantly saved by *guardian angels*. The numerous near-death experiences accounted for dozens of fractured bones and rendered the author unconscious on five separate occasions, yet he somehow lived to tell his compelling story. After reading this account, one's view of life, one's apprehension of death, and one's belief in angels will never be the same again.

    All praise and honor to our God in his glory,
for His will shall be done thus never to worry.
You can make the world a better place for all,
so simply stop taking up space before the fall.
Express life with a bountiful joy and a zest,
nine lives to eternity reflects our Lord is best.
    —Scott D. Gottschalk (2010)

Terrifying Tales Unleashed
Unsettling Stories to Remedy Peaceful Slumber

Terrifying Tales Unleashed is a menagerie of short stories covering many popular genres including horror, science fiction, and suspense/thriller. Cover the gamut in this gripping narrative by way of buried alive, rats, bats, vampires, werewolves, zombies, aliens, ghosts, demons, and cannibals. The unleashing of each twisted account will bombard one's thoughts with impending shock waves. Will you be able to hold on to your own reality? Can you make yourself believe that what you are about to read is nothing more than a few tall tales? Are you prepared to partake in a remedy for peaceful slumber and succumb to fitful nights of insomnia? The stories within this book are nothing more than pure fiction and certainly could not have really happened. OR COULD THEY?

    Although these short tales may be ever so brief,
The terror and fear shall only cause grief.
Prepare for the worst and protect one's heart,
For in the end perhaps death may you part!
    —Scott D. Gottschalk (2011)

NO BOUNDARIES TOUR

I have come to realize that I may not be right in the head, however I am completely fine with that idea.
—Scott D. Gottschalk (2023)

Make no little plans. They have no
magic to stir men's blood.
—Daniel Burnham (1909)

I tried to be normal once,
worst two minutes of my life
—Author Unknown

Life is made up of two dates and a dash,
make the most of the dash.
—Author Unknown

This book is dedicated to every family member, valued friend, gracious sponsor, benevolent donor, and the many supportive volunteers, including the international membership of the Christian Motorcycle Association (CMA) and the international membership of Bikers Against Child Abuse (BACA).

Your selfless dedication, commitment, passion, and prayers provided the impetus for the success of the No Boundaries Tour Charity to Fight Human Trafficking. You have played an important role to make a difference for those who suffer from this plight.

Lastly, a special dedication to all the ordinary people who accomplish extraordinary achievements while doing their time on planet Earth. Choose to ignore the countless negative feedback that emits from the mouths of many and instead pursue one's loftiest ambitions with the gusto it deserves. Those who dwell in the conventional lanes, typically believe that since they are incapable of such achievements, then surely the atypical personality can't make such an accomplishment either. That is total BS, so I urge you to go ahead and reach for your outer limits!

UNDERSTANDING HUMAN TRAFFICKING

Criterion: The bound victim depicted on the front cover is not typically what human trafficking looks like in today's world, thus making it difficult to identify.

Blue Campaign is a national public awareness campaign designed to educate the public, law enforcement, and other industry partners to recognize the indicators of human trafficking and how to appropriately respond to possible cases.

Blue Campaign works closely with DHS Components to develop general awareness trainings as well as specific educational resources to help reduce victimization within vulnerable populations.
    Located within the DHS Center for Countering Human Trafficking, Blue Campaign leverages partnerships with the private sector, nongovernmental organizations (NGO), law enforcement, and state/local authorities to maximize national public engagement on anti-human trafficking efforts. Blue Campaign's educational awareness objectives consists of two foundational elements, prevention of human trafficking and protection of exploited persons.

What Is Human Trafficking?

Human trafficking involves the use of force, fraud, or coercion to obtain some type of labor or commercial sex act. Every year, millions of men, women, and children are trafficked worldwide—including right here in the United States. It can happen in any community and victims can be any age, race, gender, or nationality. Traffickers might use the following methods to lure victims into trafficking situations:

- Violence
- Manipulation
- False promises of well-paying jobs
- Romantic relationships

Language barriers, fear of their traffickers, and/or fear of law enforcement frequently keep victims from seeking help, making human trafficking a hidden crime.

Traffickers look for people who are easy targets for a variety of reasons, including:

- Psychological or emotional vulnerability
- Economic hardship
- Lack of a social safety net
- Natural disasters
- Political instability

The trauma caused by the traffickers can be so great that many may not identify themselves as victims or ask for help, even in highly public settings. Many myths and misconceptions exist. Recognizing key indicators of human trafficking is the first step in identifying victims and can help save a life. Not all indicators listed are present in every human trafficking situation, and the presence or absence of any of the indicators is not necessarily proof of human trafficking. The safety of the public as well as the victim is important. Do not attempt to confront a suspected trafficker directly or alert a victim to any suspicions. It is up to law enforcement to investigate suspected cases of human trafficking.

Indicators of Human Trafficking

Recognizing key indicators of human trafficking is the first step in identifying victims and can help save a life. Here are some common indicators to help recognize human trafficking.

- Does the person appear disconnected from family, friends, community organizations, or houses of worship?
- Has a child stopped attending school?
- Has the person had a sudden or dramatic change in behavior?
- Is a juvenile engaged in commercial sex acts?
- Is the person disoriented or confused or showing signs of mental or physical abuse?
- Does the person have bruises in various stages of healing?
- Is the person fearful, timid, or submissive?
- Does the person show signs of having been denied food, water, sleep, or medical care?
- Is the person often in the company of someone to whom he or she defers? Or someone who seems to be in control of the situation, e.g., where they go or who they talk to?
- Does the person appear to be coached on what to say?
- Is the person living in unsuitable conditions?
- Does the person lack personal possessions and appear not to have a stable living situation?
- Does the person have freedom of movement? Can the person freely leave where they live? Are there unreasonable security measures?

Not all indicators listed above are present in every human trafficking situation, and the presence or absence of any of the indicators is not necessarily proof of human trafficking.

See. Call. Save.

Do not at any time attempt to confront a suspected trafficker directly or alert a victim to your suspicions. Your safety as well as the victim's safety is paramount. Instead, please contact local law enforcement directly or call the tip lines indicated on this page:

Call 1-866-DHS-2-ICE (1-866-347-2423) to report suspicious criminal activity to the U.S. Immigration and Customs Enforcement (ICE) Homeland Security Investigations (HSI) Tip Line 24 hours a day, 7 days a week, every day of the year. Highly trained specialists take reports from both the public and law enforcement agencies on more than 400 laws enforced by ICE HSI, including those related to human trafficking. The tip line is accessible **outside the United States** by calling 802-872-6199.

To get help from the National Human Trafficking Hotline (NHTH), call 1-888-373-7888 **or text HELP or INFO to BeFree (233733).** The NHTH can help connect victims with service providers in the area and provides training, technical assistance, and other resources. The NHTH is a national toll-free hotline available to answer calls from anywhere in the country, 24 hours a day, 7 days a week, every day of the year. The NHTH is not a law enforcement or immigration authority and is operated by a nongovernmental organization funded by the Federal Government.

By identifying victims and reporting tips, you are doing your part to help law enforcement rescue victims, and you might save a life. Law enforcement can connect victims to services such as medical and mental health care, shelter, job training, and legal assistance that restore their freedom and dignity. The presence or absence of any of the indicators is not necessarily proof of human trafficking. It is up to law enforcement to investigate suspected cases of human trafficking.

PROLOGUE

What intrinsic element lies within the complex human spirit that allows a handful of individuals to set outlandish benchmarks and miraculous goals and then they somehow find it deep within themselves to reach those unbelievable expectations?

As opposed to those who set their bars so high that few can fathom their achievements, we then know there also lies the sinister elements that fabricates within other complex human beings to seek out the worst that humankind can offer.

This then is the premise for this story and this journey that defines both extremes in human behavior from the encouraging side to the opposing destructive perspective. This story first began from a young age revolving around a sincere love of riding motorcycles. The persistent yearning to ride free and in the elements unlike no other confined motorized vehicle could offer or duplicate. That love of motorcycles developed into a lifelong quest to cover longer and longer distances yearning to experience the soothing, relaxing joy of riding. Out there somewhere were some potential record-breaking motorcycling rides to possibly be earned and quite conceivably for a very good cause, if only to be discovered.

It became an obsession for me to attempt to break a couple of iconic motorcycle long-distance world records.

At the writing of this book, the current Guiness Book of World Records Ride: longest journey by motorcycle in a single country (individual) was achieved from April 3 to August 5, 2022, by Dana D'Arcy. She rode her 2020 Harley-Davidson Road Glide Limited motorcycle an incredible 82,598 miles in 125 days. Dana took a four-month sabbatical from her career as a certified registered nurse anesthetist in South Florida to experience her once-in-a-lifetime motorcycle trip.

She averaged over 660 miles per day and only missed two days of riding the entire time due to a shredded drive belt.

At the writing of this book, another separate world record has been established for the Iron Butt Association (IBA) Long-Distance Motorcycle Riding World Record. This record has been dubbed the "Saddle Sore 100,000" and covered 100,454 miles in 100 consecutive days of riding through all 48 contiguous states. This new record shattered the previous legendary long-distance rider Matt Wise's 45,000 miles in 45 days IBA World Record. The remarkable latest world record was achieved by Chris Hopper from Texas whose ride went from July 27 to November 4, 2021, riding on his 2021 Harley-Davidson Road Glide Limited motorcycle. Not only did Chris set the new Motorcycle Distance Record, but he also raised more than $100,000 to benefit those with Duchenne Muscular Dystrophy (DMD), a genetic disorder that causes progressive muscle degeneration, usually among young boys.

So, there it is, two amazing Motorcycle Riding World Records, waiting for the next goal-setting dreamer to step up for a good fundraising campaign. From May to September of 2025, the "No Boundaries Tour Ride" will utilize a new 120th Year Harley-Davidson Anniversary 2023 Harley-Davidson Road Glide Limited motorcycle to accomplish a new combined Guinness Record and Iron Butt Association Record by running +120,000 miles, in under 120 days, and help raise $1.2 million in funds to bring awareness to and help fight human trafficking and sexual exploitation.

Therein lies the ultimate compassion for the success of this record attempt. Let it be known that our United States has a top-ranking in the world for an exceptionally negative and sinister reason. The United States of America is currently ranked the #1 most human trafficking and sex trafficking nation of the world! Unbelievably, human trafficking earns global profits of roughly $150 billion a year for traffickers, of which $99 billion comes directly from commercial sexual exploitation. This is a ghastly record that no one should accept, and the No Boundaries Tour Ride intends to make a dent in this disgusting reality. Please be a part of the solution and help us fight to stop this insanity that affects so many of our abducted underage girls and boys, not only in our country but worldwide.

In summary, what intrinsic element lies within the complex human spirit that allows a handful of individuals to set outlandish positive benchmarks with miraculous goals, and then they somehow find it deep within themselves to reach those unbelievable expectations?

Why then do others set their bars so low that few can fathom their downfall? The sinister elements that fabricate within these other complex human beings to seek out the worst that humankind can offer is undeniable.

Let's ride, let's live, let's make a difference, let's bring awareness to this scourge on humankind, and let's fight back against this worsening plaque on humankind! Are you willing to push your boundaries, or will you pass through life, as so many, regretting the rides you didn't take?

EACH ONE OF US CAN IMPLEMENT THE
LEGACY TO BE REMEMBERED.

INTRODUCTION

Growing up as a child on a labor-intensive livestock and grain farm in southeastern Minnesota gave me the essence and direction to set the course for my entire life. It was on that farm with my strong Christian upbringing where my parents, my siblings, and I toiled endless hours each day trying to scratch out the barest of an existence from the land. That was not only our farm-family's mission in life but was the mission in life of countless other farm families in their inspirational effort to feed the masses of humankind on our increasingly populated planet.

As a direct result of my rural upbringing, what became instilled in my makeup was a strong work ethic, a dedication, and a commitment to succeed that has remained with me my entire life.

It was during my high school days that I once set a lofty goal to one day write a book. The impetus behind this dream of writing a book came because of the several hours each week that I spent reading nearly every book, which I could lay my hands upon.

My favorite book topics at the time revolved around stories about animals. The endless hours that I spent reading these kinds of books one day eventually helped lead to my lifelong career path in animal agriculture. Just as importantly, reading so many books in those youthful days eventually drove my dream and desire to write my first book, which was filled with animal stories based upon my own personal experiences while growing up on the farm.

Back then, to prepare for that task of becoming an author and to hone my book-writing skills, I began taking extra writing elective courses while still in high school. This brought on a lot of questionable comments from my friends and teachers, but I'd made the decision to secretly keep my objective that I would one day author and hopefully publish a book.

Following my high school graduation, I enrolled in college at the University of Minnesota where I eventually obtained my double bachelor of science degree in both agriculture education and animal science. During those busy college years, I kept my secretive book-writing dream alive, yet I received many challenges from my agriculture classmates, when they discovered that I was taking so many elective courses in English and writing courses.

At the time, whenever I was asked why I was taking so many non-agriculture-major courses by my classmates, I simply replied, "I really like English and writing-related topics." This was not exactly giving them the entire story, but I simply didn't want to claim that I aspired to write a book one day, only to then spend the rest of my life answering the question of "When do you think you will complete the book?" "Is it done yet?" "Are you finished yet?" "Are you ever going to finish it?"

Through a lot of diligence and perseverance, I was able to complete my first attempt at writing a book shortly after my graduation from college. It didn't take too long, and I was hit with the "speed of life" while I began my new career, began my marriage to my wife, Astrid, and we started our family.

Somehow in all the rush of those early days of my young adulthood, I found the fortitude to finish my first book-writing project, and *The Folk and Their Fauna* was published in 1982. Suddenly at a mere twenty-six years of age, I was in the whirlwind of the experiences resulting from becoming a first-time published author. While writing my first book was a tremendous experience, I pledged at that time that writing one and only one book was more than enough authoring experience in my entire lifetime. It had taken a bunch of discipline and my 100% commitment to reach that goal. Enough of that notion already!

Fast-forward more than forty years, amazingly I've pounded out a fourth book on my keyboard. I've been so blessed in my lifetime to experience so much that life has to offer. I'm eternally grateful to been lauded with the gift of storytelling.

From my perspective, I personally feel that within each human lies an amazing story or tale of some kind. I believe that most everyone could write a book of some consequence from within their own unique set of circumstances and life experiences. The real challenge, however, is that no matter how many individuals dream of writing their own book, and many do dream this dream, the basic truth is that a minuscule few will ever actually reach such an objective.

Few people could ever imagine the passion and dedication it takes to compile a story into a book format. Even fewer "wishful authors" can even comprehend the challenges it takes to get one's story published. Finally, after one invests endless hours preparing, note-taking, writing, rewriting, editing, and finally publishing a potential book, then ultimately someone out there must want to buy it to read it.

The title I chose for this my fourth book is *No Boundaries Tour: The Fight Against Human Trafficking*. Now, let me take you on a literary journey to accomplish a world record motorcycle ride charity fundraiser. Hang on because this will not be for the faint of heart.

I've concluded that God's plan for me is somehow not yet finished. I passionately believe that the Lord has a mission for me, and until my job on this earth is finished, I will not be called to my heavenly Creator no matter how much danger my life handles. For this reason, I'm completely convinced that my Lord and Savior have blessed me with a message that needs to be shared through the words of this book.

I've not only been given this opportunity through the pages of this book to share these wonders with you, but I've been blessed with whatever stubbornness, perseverance, and commitment that it might take to get this message out to you.

    I pray that your faith and your beliefs be forevermore strengthened.

CHAPTER 1
Driven by Competitive Nature

In the 1950s, my father was a highly ranked high school wrestler. He was so skilled that no one was able to score a single point against him his entire senior year of high school. Although he was granted an Olympic tryout and was even offered a four-year college scholarship to continue wrestling in college, he chose instead to get married at the age of 18, become a dairy farmer, and start a family.

By the time my brother Jerry was age three and I was age six, we were given wrestling mats for our Christmas gift that year. Long before we had honed many other skills, we were adept at doing takedowns and putting in strong pinning combinations on defenseless opponents. At that time, the sport of wrestling seemed just okay to me, but it came across in my eyes as a very difficult sport that didn't lend itself much to having fun. What do I mean, you might ask? Well, take some of the ball sports, baseball, basketball, football, or volleyball. Not only are they fun spectator sports, but as true team events, the athletes seem to really have fun participating during their competitions. Now let's compare those to wrestling. Wrestling is primarily an individual sport where one competitor faces off against another, all alone in front of the crowd. One must go up against that opponent basically doing legalized hand-to-hand combat for their entire wrestling match. Ironically, anything to do with wrestling is never called a game, which I liken to doing something fun, but rather they are called wrestling matches.

Bottom line, my brother and I figured other sports might be easier, so we informed our father that we'd like to try another sport. He quite matter-of-factly let us know that since our dairy farm and cropping enterprises would not allow for either of us to be in a fall or a springtime sport, then choosing a winter sport was going to be our sole option. Our father then enforced the point when he informed us that he didn't consider any other winter sport reason enough to get out of our wintertime milking and farming chores, except for wrestling of course. He offered that he didn't care if we decided to become wrestlers or not, but if not, we would then be expected to do our work on the farm without further complaints. Ultimately, my brother and I liked the idea of wrestling much better than milking cows every day, so wrestle we did.

In time, as adults, we married and had children of our own. When my two sons were very young and considering the sport of wrestling, I asked that they consider instead some team sports that played with some kind of ball. I was promptly informed that they wanted to stay with family tradition and become wrestlers. Today, I'm blessed with seven grandchildren, and there is now a fourth generation of wrestlers. Considering my background, I wasn't surprised to find that I spent much of my time wrestling with all things and everyone. I'm convinced that someone who spends years of their existence in a grappling sport, loves confrontation and doing battle to some extent. The path that I set forth at an early age was simply heading me straight for a life of chaos, mischief, danger, and sin. All who knew me worried for my future, and those who loved me wondered what it would take to bring some moderation into my life. I blindly set forth on a path of self-destruction with little regard for those around me. During those times, I simply refused to buy in to moderation of any sort. My parents grew weary of my antics of always too fast and always too reckless. I spent far too much of my school years taking pride in causing trouble for so many of my teachers and the others who cared about me.

There could be no doubt that I was out of control and destined for trouble beyond description if something didn't change. My adrenaline-filled pathway was leading me toward either jail or death or perhaps both! I was living on the edge looking for some missing piece in my life, trying to determine my purpose in life.

As I've journeyed throughout my life, at times, I've often wrestled with the idea should one fight every war, or should one do a better job of picking one's battles?

Now let me share a couple of my memorable life-wrestling matches I was lucky to survive but, eventually, helped me find the solutions to my purpose in life.

Many times, throughout my life, I've made some very poor decisions. Like all human beings, I've committed sins; and in my younger years, some of those extreme sins even landed me in jail. Later in life as I matured, I realized at a point in my life that moving from a continuous sinful path toward more acts of good was something to strive for. I made a commitment to "turn over a new leaf" and became an international agriculture consultant. For more than three decades, and for much of my adult life, I've wondered if that was my true life's mission.

Over the years, I've invested over six months providing services in several dangerous underdeveloped nations, oftentimes in harm's way. I reasoned that if I used the gifts and talents given me, such work might hopefully make the world just a little bit better place for all and perhaps that would surely put things right with my life. As a result of some of those assignments, I found an inner strength never known to exist. My life was saved on several occasions including surviving a bombing explosion in Afghanistan, protecting me from a tragic car accident in Poland, and providing the miracle that kept me from certain death during a mass riot in Africa where I witnessed several lives lost. Still, I wrestled with who am I, and what is the grand plan?

A very different life-affirming activity came about from a catastrophic motorcycle accident that nearly claimed my life a few years ago. I've been a daredevil and adrenaline junkie for much of my life, so I often select "bucket list" experiences that most others likely avert. That crash came about because of an attempt to certify and ride a long-distance 3,000-mile cross-country attempt. That ride was cut short when I hit a deer. As I recovered from that horrific accident, which resulted in countless broken bones, a broken back in three places, and several required surgeries, I once again questioned my mission in life. I often wondered if helping impoverished people of the world was the course I should take or was there something else pointing the way. During struggling with those injuries and many surgeries, I believe a clear message came at last.

This brings me to my most recent and profound personal wrestling match. After such a severe motorcycle crash a few years earlier, I'd made promises to my family to no longer risk life and limb on such extreme endurance motorcycle rides. I kept that promise for a few years, but eventually the thrill and excitement became too strong as I was drawn once again into the web of another extreme ride. I aspired to become the first to ride a motorcycle continuously in all 50 states in under 10 days. Sounds impossible, but I was convinced it could be done. My wife asked me why, and my response was that I'd rather live life to the fullest rather than die dreaming of what might have been. With reservations, my family accepted my choice to proceed. Countless times, I prayed to God asking Him for a sign of guidance or direction. In my prayers, I asked that if my life was to be terminated then I was okay with going home to His eternal kingdom as the final step in His salvation. Some of those prayers also asked if because of making such an attempt, God might provide more opportunities to share His glorious message with others. God made that choice for me on a lonely stretch of highway, and this story was the result.

Let me share some the challenging aspects of such a nearly impossible motorcycle journey. The basics of certifying the endurance ride meant that I had to park my motorcycle at the Minneapolis Airport and then fly to Hawaii. Once in Hawaii, a rental motorcycle was used to then log 50 miles officially in Hawaii. The next stage of the journey required an immediate flight back to the Minneapolis Airport while still on the time clock from the Hawaii leg of the trip. I then had the daunting task of attempting to ride a motorcycle across the remaining 48 continental United States before finally ending the ride in the state of Alaska under the ten-day limit.

Although I ultimately came up one state short, God ventured along with me while successfully covering 49 states and riding more than nine thousand miles in a mere seven days. How could it be done one might ask? Well, the logistics required twenty-two hours per day nonstop riding time while leaving only two hours per night for sleep. Hour after hour, day after long day, I pushed on, but all the while I felt myself growing ever closer to God. As the miles elapsed, I drew comfort knowing that I had countless family, friends, and prayer groups whose prayers combined with my own prayers asking for God's love and mercy on me. I came to believe that God loved me as I'd never discovered before. Sometime during the middle stages of this ride, I became acutely aware that wrestling with God doesn't serve much purpose.

Due to some punishing traveling challenges between the fifth- and sixth-day segments of the ride, I was unfortunately forced to ride an entire forty-eight-hour period without the much-needed two-hour motel rest. In that long stretch of riding, the twelve states of Georgia, Alabama, Florida, Mississippi, Louisiana, Arkansas, Texas, Oklahoma, Missouri, Kansas, Colorado, and New Mexico were canvassed before finally stopping.

It was during the long westward ride across Kansas on I-70 that I came to understand the power and love of God. I was exhausted as I'd never been. I've never fallen asleep on a motorcycle before, but after all the hours and all the miles and all the lack of sleep, my body could endure no more. I had been driving at the posted speed of seventy-five mph when I slumped over and fell asleep. Let it be said that once a driver is no longer in control of their motorcycle, very bad crashes are likely to occur shortly thereafter. I'm still in amazement with the outcome. While I was slumped over fast asleep on a racing motorcycle, I believe that God or his guardian angels surrounded and protected me while keeping that motorcycle upright and traveling straight. Experience would suggest that it should have veered either to the right or to the left and ultimately caused an accident, yet the bike stayed driving true as if still under control. The bike eventually slowed to about thirty-five mph when I awoke because of the noisy vehicles racing past me.

At that moment, I knew I was in trouble as I prayed out loud saying, "Lord, I'm in your hands. Am I to live or die?" At that very instant, a Rest Stop sign suddenly appeared from nowhere, as I veered into that rest stop. Still shaking from what had just happened, I parked my motorcycle, went up to a concrete picnic table, and collapsed flat out on top of it. Before losing consciousness from total exhaustion, I spoke aloud to God and said, "Lord, I'm at your mercy if I'm to complete this test of endurance, then I leave it all up to you. Thank you for watching over me Heavenly Father."

In exactly thirty minutes, I awoke more rested and refreshed than ever before. Without delay, I was back on the motorcycle riding across Kansas. At that moment, I felt a closeness with God such as I'd never experienced in my lifetime. I felt protected with the surreal warmth of being surrounded by his love. Up ahead, a massive thunderstorm was about to strike and under most circumstances, whenever rain occurs, most bikers simply pull off the road to put on their rain gear and then continue onward. This time, for the strangest reason, I continued my dialogue with God saying, "God, you undoubtedly saved my life when I fell asleep on the highway. Now rather than put a rainsuit, I'm instead going to drive straight through this rainstorm and let you baptize me in your cleansing rain." Surging through the storm getting bitterly cold and soaked, I once more conversed with God asking why He couldn't just occasionally prove he exists to us mere mortals.

I asked, "Couldn't you just make it easier for us down on earth to once in a great while just show us a sign that you really do exist?" Now I know that God in all his glory never needs to prove anything to we as His children, yet what was about to happen changed me forever!

About that time off in the distance of the massive thunderstorm, I spotted a lone semitruck traveling at a slower pace through the rain about three miles ahead of me on the same side of the highway. I looked upwards believing that God was in full command and said, "You know, by the time I reach that semitruck, it would sure be nice if you would turn off the faucet of this frigid storm and bring the sunshine back out." Several minutes later, I was catching up to the semitruck and just as the front wheel of my motorcycle inched past the rear of the semitruck, the rain instantly ceased, the pavement was dry, and the sun broke out into a glorious day! Was that just a coincidence? In my heart, I don't feel there are any coincidences with God, but rather I believe that God orchestrates each and everything within His plan.

At that moment, I wept as I've never wept before. In that instant, I was overwhelmed and humbled to know that the God of the entire universe would bring about such an unbelievable change in conditions to remind me of His great love. It felt as though God had reached out and touched me in a way that would never leave me in doubt again of His existence. My hope swelled and my belief in God strengthened as never before. At that moment, I felt a surreal sense of love and protection from God that is difficult for me to describe. I'd started out on an amazing motorcycle journey all full of myself and initially believing I would be applauded for such an achievement, yet my paltry efforts were paled by comparison to the heroics of God!

Sometime a couple of days later, my final phone call home from my trip went out to my wife at 3:00 a.m. from a desolate highway north of Seattle, Washington, with the final state of Alaska looming just ahead to complete my 50-state marathon motorcycle ride. My wife held her breath as I shared on that call, "With another miracle from God, I've just survived another motorcycle crash. I believe that God wanted this trip to end for me with just one state of journey remaining." I described to my wife how I'd been glancing at my GPS when the bike veered into the ditch and was destroyed while flipping several times. God answered those many prayers by saving my life as the 900-pound motorcycle landed directly on top of my head breaking my helmet, yet I didn't have a mark on my body and absolutely no injuries! Through her tears, my wife shared that when she said her goodbyes to me just prior to the start of my ride, her prayers to God never ceased, and yet she'd been fearful of never again seeing me alive. She breathed a huge sigh of relief when I explained, "As soon as I dispose of the motorcycle in a salvage yard, I'm flying back home. Please plan to pick me up at the airport back home in a few hours."

As previously stated, I've spent much of my life living on the edge and taking enormous risks. For most of my life, I've been a hard-driving, danger-seeking, "guys' guy." Thankfully, I've discovered some moderation in my life, and I no longer crave the chaos, mischief, self-destruction, and trouble-causing antics that once were such a driving force. What hasn't changed is I'm still a fast-paced thrill seeker who still enjoys experiencing the many things that is before us on this earth.

Yes, I'd accepted Christ into my heart years ago, but I was all too often in a continual wrestling match with God, all full of myself and constantly challenging His will. In time, I've turned the controls of my life over to Jesus with his promise to grant eternal life in paradise. It has become clearer to me who Jesus Christ is. Jesus is the One who takes away our sin. Try as we may, we are still human sinners throughout our lifetimes. Jesus is the Son of God who took the punishment for our sin, dying on the cross, yet rising again that those of us who believe might have eternal life and become His children.

My message in this chapter is that I'm nothing more than a common person who is deeply comforted by my faith. For much of my life, I've wrestled with God and so many others. On several occasions, I have been humbled, amazed, and awestruck by God's mighty acts of divine intervention. In every situation, God's loving presence stayed true. In my past, I've run away from Him, but God caught me on that lonely highway while riding a motorcycle and this time I'm conceding my eternal soul to the true victor once and for all. As my life has unfolded, I've been comforted by the loving patience of God. At times I've ignored Him, many times I've wandered away, but no matter how far I've strayed, the Lord has always been there with me every step of the way. This is regardless of our acknowledging our need for Him or not.

As my life has unfolded, I'm extremely driven by my competitive nature. All that being indicated, one may now have a better understanding for my drive to set a new world record motorcycle ride.

CHAPTER 2

Motorcycling Love Affair

Motorcycling has been one of my greater passions throughout life, which just so happens to also be a primary cause for eight of my closest encounters with death. In all, during my lifetime, I've dealt with the aftermath of eight significant motorcycling accidents, but it was the fourth wreck, which I'll cover in a later chapter, that left me at the very brink of death while suffering from the most severe injuries I'd ever incurred. In the following story, though, I'll review my initial motorcycling collision that began it all.

Growing up and living in the countryside with our home alongside a dusty rural gravel road made our travels into town a rather bumpy and dirty affair. Our rickety older model cars or our farm pickup trucks would rumble and groan each time we scampered off to town for something. While I was growing up, I had a strong fascination for motorcycles. Invariably, once our unsavory vehicles would make their way along our rural roads and onto the more modern highways, we would oftentimes witness the carefree expression of a passing motorcyclist racing by us.

From an early age, I was awestruck by how agile and snappy these motorbikes were. They almost appeared to my young impressionable eyes as though they were big two-wheeled mosquitoes capable of darting in and out of traffic with reckless abandon and ease. To my way of thinking, the motorcycles were certainly a more remarkable form of transportation than were our lumbering farm vehicles that we occasionally ventured into town with. My ears would perk up each time a passing biker would roll the grip of their hand throttle and I'd be spellbound by the instant acceleration of the machine and hear the thunder coming from the tailpipes.

No matter how thrilled I became each time a motorcycle passed by, my father would in turn get ever more angry toward the bikers. My father would always go into a rant by shouting, "Those damned crazy idiots have no idea that they are all going to end up dead or in a hospital if they keep riding those death machines."

I questioned my father's commentary only once and knew better than to ever bring the topic up again when I'd asked, "Gee, Dad, what is the big deal? Motorcycles are so fast and so cool."

Without taking a breath, my father gave me one of his most profound arguments. With my father's secondary job working the night shift for the Mayo Clinic, he was always on call with the emergency room. Whenever there was a vehicular accident of any kind, he and a certain group of other medical specialists would be summoned in a hurry to perform their specific duties. Throughout our childhoods, my father never failed to remind my siblings and me just how many heartrending motorcycling accident victims he'd been required to work on over the years. My father would unleash a tirade on us kids sitting in our car whenever he'd spot a motorcycle zipping along the highway.

He would point out how the biker was speeding along only inches from the roadway without the benefit of a metal reinforced frame or even the advantage of an enclosed car body to surround the operator with some lifesaving safety features. Next, he would explain that without any seat belts or airbags, a motorcyclist was simply a death statistic waiting to happen. He could never understand what drove them to live so close to the edge of sensibility.

My father's so-called words of wisdom left a strong impact on my younger siblings, but his words fell on my deaf ears. The more my father complained about how senseless and dangerous he felt motorcycle riding was, the more I fantasized about the sheer joy of nearly floating through the air while traveling at high speeds suspended only inches above the racing roadway beneath. My father would really get rattled whenever he'd see a helmetless motorcyclist pass by our vehicle. That sight alone would turn my father into a fire-breathing dragon. He would shake his head from side to side in disbelief and sigh loudly, as he questioned why such fools would not only risk their lives on such death machines, but then do so without even wearing a precautionary safety helmet.

It became all too obvious to everyone in our family that our father was becoming more and more deeply troubled as time passed along from his personal witness to all the catastrophic motorcycling injuries he faced on a regular basis inside the emergency rooms of the hospital. I'm sure there is only so much mutilation, pain, and human suffering that any one person can absorb before it takes a stressful toll. Our father felt that if he preached his message hard enough, long enough, and often enough, he could steer his children away from dangers that motorcycling could possibly inflict upon them.

My father had a pretty good success ratio inflicting his motorcycling beliefs on his children, however, one of his five children seemed incoherent to such words of wisdom. Which one of his five offspring would one guess? Well, if you guessed me, then yes, I desired a motorcycle with everything within my being. Anything that could go fast enough to take one's breath away was enough exhilaration to spur my desires.

Whenever I could, I'd read motorcycling magazines in our high school library. I became a "closet motorbike" admirer, and during my teen years, I became a human encyclopedia of motorcycle knowledge and trivia facts. No one could stump me when it came to motorcycle facts and figures. With ease, I could spell out exactly which motorcycle model would have which size engine with what top-end speed it could achieve and, furthermore, sell for exactly what price tag, etc.

I became the envy of my friends, and everyone (except for my father) knew that it would only be matter of time and I would one day become a true biker. There was only one slight problem.

My father has always been a strong-willed and strict disciplinarian parent. Within our household, his will and direction always became a fact that could not be challenged.

My father was certainly very astute in realizing his inability to take away my obsession of one day owning and operating a motorcycle, but he made it CRYSTAL CLEAR to me on many an occasion by saying, "Scott, no child of mine will ever own or operate a motorcycle while living under my roof and while under my care." My father would always rattle on further by stating, "Someday you will grow up, you will become an adult, and then you will have my blessings to do whatever you desire, but until that day arrives, you must respect my demands at this time of your life."

The message was clear, and my respect for obeying my father's wishes was never in question. For his reasons and because of the demons he struggled with, I never let on just how much of a student of motorcycling I'd become by my late teen years. By the time I'd reached the age of seventeen, though, I already knew exactly when and how I would enter the world of motorcycle ownership. I'd laid out a specific plan for which I knew all the details ranging from which brand of motorbike to how much horsepower would sit beneath my legs to exactly how fast my cycle would travel once I finally acquired it.

I'm sure that my parents were all too aware that their rebellious son would one day move on into the fast and the furious world of motorcycling, but they never stopped hoping that I would one day come to my senses on the matter. Out of the total respect, which I've always held with both of my parents, I kept the subject of my passion for cycling hidden to myself for years.

In time, I reached the age of eighteen, graduated from high school, and moved out of my parent's household and on to college. Having reached young adulthood at last and having recently moved into my college apartment, I immediately purchased a used midsized motorcycle. In no time at all, I'd passed my written motorcycle exam, then passed my motorcycle driving test, and suddenly I was legally able to ride the machine of my dreams.

Although my father was not happy when he found out that I finally owned a motorcycle, he was somewhat comforted because I chose to wear a safety helmet while operating the motorbike. I noted a twisted smirk arise from the corner of his mouth when he shared, "At least you'll have some hope of surviving an accident if you wear your brain bucket over your head."

It is difficult to describe my initial experience with my motorcycle. I remember shaking with delight as I mounted the sleek and racy machine. With a quick turn of the key, I brought the roar of its throaty engine to life for the first time. With a downward click of the foot gear shifter, I engaged the transmission, and with the release of the left hand clutch, my motorcycle and I sped off for the very first time. I'd liken it to one's first kiss or perhaps one's first love. It was simply an unforgettable experience, which I've treasured always and whose memory never fades.

For my entire life, I've been drawn to anything that makes my heart race and takes my breath away. As I raced along the highways on that virgin motorcycle ride, I experienced an unbelievable joy as the bike and I became as one. We leaned together while twisting quickly and easily through curves in the roads with a feeling such as I'd never experienced before. With merely a slight twist of my right throttle grip, the two-wheeled machine ratcheted up its speed in an instant.

Riding a motorcycle for the first time left me with an insatiable desire to never want to give up such a feeling of pure, unadulterated freedom and joy. How could something so wonderful create so much disdain from my father was beyond me?

It was summertime, and I'd just moved my meager belongings away from my beloved room inside my parent's home and which I'd shared with my brother Jerry for so many years then relocated everything to my apartment about one hundred miles away in the metropolitan mega of Minneapolis. I had been in such a hurry to reach adulthood and to acquire a motorcycle of my own. I moved away that summer without so much as looking back and instantly began working a summer job in my effort to earn some college tuition funds. When fall arrived that year, I began my classes at the University of Minnesota after surviving a few months of big-city dwelling.

Each day I rode my motorcycle to and from my temporary job. I was in so much ecstasy riding it that rain or shine, cold or warm, I rode then rode it some more. It didn't take long to figure out the benefits of motorcycle ownership for a young college student. For starters, the motorbike only sipped gasoline by achieving well over fifty miles per gallon, which really helped me with low-cost travels. With its maneuverability, I could move in and out of the congested big-city traffic with an ease such as I'd never experienced before. Finally, with such a petite size, I was always capable of parking my cycle anywhere and everywhere, which could not so easily have been accomplished with larger cars and pickup trucks.

I'd become quite accustomed to the advantages of motorcycle ownership as summer evolved into fall and I began my first college courses. Most of the other college students' rode buses to and from college each day. A few students had a vehicle of some sort to drive, but it was a rare few of us that in fact possessed a motorcycle to maneuver about campus and travel the city.

Living away from our farm and suddenly dwelling within the big city while attending college was not an easy adjustment for me at first. I was all too aware of the sheer numbers of people all around. How different it was living within the city where one could hear sounds and voices emanating from every direction inside of one's apartment versus the quiet solitude inside of our farmhouse. The mass of vehicles and hurried pace of the city made for a difficult transition for me.

Without doubt, upon moving to the city, I became somewhat suspicious and mistrusting of my belongings. So much so that each evening as I parked my motorcycle at my apartment, I would secure it with a large chain and padlock it to one of the large metal security light poles in the parking lot of the apartment complex where I lived. At night, I could always sleep better, knowing that I had removed my ignition keys, then locked the front forks of my motorbike, then chained and locked it securely before walking away.

This methodology of protecting my new motorcycle worked wonderfully for the first couple of months. One morning, however, I arose early for my summertime job, showered, and dressed, then headed out into the parking lot to ready my motorbike for my hasty departure. Suddenly I stopped in my tracks as I investigated the empty parking space where my cycle had been safely secured. Only the severed large chain remained where it was still wrapped around the large security light pole, which I'd mistakenly believed could protect my bike.

In a matter of moments, I called the area law enforcement department to report that my much-adored motorcycle had been stolen. I angrily waited until the two Minneapolis policemen knocked at my door and stepped into my apartment. After providing a detailed statement for their police report and divulging everything I could regarding my motorcycle, they stood up preparing to leave. As I walked them to the door, I asked how long they felt it might take before my precious motorcycle would be found, the thief who stole it arrested and incarcerated, and then my bike returned to me.

The policemen burst out into laughter when they announced, "Son, you must have grown up somewhere in the sticks because your motorcycle has probably already been parted out overnight and is being sold for motorcycle parts as we speak!"

I felt my face flush with anger as I responded back by saying, "Well, there must be some chance of getting my machine back, isn't there?"

Again, I drew a chuckle from the cops as they responded, "Look, it would be best for you to simply turn this theft over to your insurance company, have them provide you with a payoff for the stolen motorcycle, then go out and buy yourself another one if you are so inclined."

With that, they marched out of my apartment and departed. I never heard from them or the police department regarding the matter of my stolen motorcycle ever again.

I sat down in disbelief at how violated I felt. How could some worthless criminal take what I'd fantasized about for so long, what I'd worked so hard for and that I'd enjoyed so heartily without even the slightest care or concern for me?

Welcome to the real-world, farm boy, I thought to myself.

I grew up a lot that day as I realized that all of God's children do not travel the same path in life, but rather good versus evil can be a prevailing theme. I was so young and so ignorant about what could transpire outside the confines of a simple and honest life on the farm.

Not to be defeated, though, I went ahead and made that call to my insurance company, and before long, I was shopping for another motorcycle. It seemed surreal that I'd only acquired my first motorcycle a short while ago, and now in less than ninety days, I was about to purchase my second motorbike. As is so often the case, after my insurance deductible was subtracted and then they calculated how much my stolen motorcycle had depreciated in value while under my ownership, I was paid only a portion of what I'd invested to purchase that first bike.

Remember that at this time, I had moved away from my home destined to pay my way through college, as well as own and operate a motorcycle. My parents did not approve of either choice but had granted me the freedom to make my own decisions as a young adult. Since asking my father for some financial help to either pay for my college costs or, worse yet, to help me purchase another motorcycle was OUT OF THE QUESTION, I went forth with my plan.

The insurance company settlement for my stolen motorcycle was a payment of about two-thirds of my original investment.

Having no additional funding at the time, I walked into a Minneapolis motorcycle business and said, "My mid-sized motorcycle has recently been stolen, and I only have enough money to cover the cost of one about two-thirds the size of my previous one."

After looking over several model designs and choices, I soon drove away on a new, yet smaller, "on-road, off-road" motorcycle. Although I had to sacrifice some size, some power, and some speed with my new sized-down bike, I had gained a nimbler, dual-purpose motorbike. Not only could I legally travel along the roads and highways, albeit at much less speed potential, but I now had a machine with high-traction tires and a tough suspension allowing me at any time could veer off the traveled highway and travel into the rough hills and trails to become one with nature during my riding experience.

Immediately after obtaining my new motorcycle, I vowed to never allow it to be stolen as had been the situation with my first bike. Beginning the first night of ownership, I parked the new motorcycle in a new location. Rather than parking it in the parking lot as before, I started parking my motorbike immediately next to the large bedroom window of my apartment. As always, before leaving my motorcycle for the evening, I would remove the ignition key and lock the front forks of the motorbike. Rather than lock and chain the bike to an immovable object, however, instead I connected a hidden wire, which I tied to the rear wheel of the motorcycle, then ran the wire through my bedroom window, and which was lastly attached to a bell inside of my bedroom. Then for the next four years of my college education, each night I slept peacefully throughout the night with a loaded automatic forty-five caliber handgun beneath my bed. I never worried again, and I had no doubt about how I would protect myself and my property from criminals when the need arose from a ringing bell inside my bedroom.

Graciously, the Lord never tested my resolve in this matter, and thankfully, neither my motorcycle nor I were ever violated again.

Before long, I had become one with my new machine and fell in love with the new feats I could complete with it. No longer was I restricted to traveling down a mundane highway. I now controlled a two-wheeler with the athletic ability to go nearly anywhere in the wilderness that a deer or perhaps even a horse could venture, only do it with more speed and excitement. With every chance I had, I would travel out to backwoods areas with my new motorcycle as I powered up hills, broke new trails, sped past ponds and rivers, and jumped high into the air with abandon. I had always loved the adrenaline rush from doing similar activities while rushing through the trees and hills with my horses, but the thrill from this new mechanized mode of trailblazing was unequaled in my mind.

In time, I became a skilled rider both on the road and off the road with my versatile new motorcycle. In no time,

I developed a timing and a balance that allowed me to maneuver my bike through the most challenging scenarios yet come away unscathed and intact. If my parents could only have known the antics, I had become accustomed in the short while since I'd owned my two different motorcycles.

It was a sunny weekend Saturday in the early fall during my first year of college. Following a long week of studies and working every evening on my part-time job during the previous week, I was prepared to finally enjoy some "me time" and to unwind from the long week. I dressed then went outside to ready my motorbike for a few hours of rough riding on the trails. First, I put on my leather motorcycle jacket, secured my helmet onto my head, inserted my hands into my thick leather riding gloves, then fired up my cycle and drove away.

After giving my motorcycle and me an extreme workout for a few of hours, I guided my bike back toward my apartment complex to end the fun time for the day. The design of my apartment complex was such that on one side of the parking lot was several apartment buildings, including the apartment which I resided in. Positioned along the other side of the parking lot was an expansive athletic field where various college intramural sporting activities took place throughout the week.

Since I was returning from riding some wilderness trails with my motorcycle, I felt that I had one more exciting "daredevil" motorcycle jump left in me before calling it a day and parking my bike. I was about to attempt the same motorcycle jump that I'd completed several times previously, but because of the dangers, I knew that I had to be careful regarding certain factors.

I quickly surveyed the entire apartment complex and made a mental note that all was quiet, both all around the apartment buildings, as well the fact that there was no one in or around the black-topped parking lot itself. I was relieved that no people were to be seen, albeit many times there were young children playing on the sidewalks or possibly a car or two would be moving about the parking lot. Had that been the case and I would have detected any movement at all, I would have aborted my last motorcycle thrill of the day.

From the road then, I jumped my motorbike over the curb, and without so much as a second notion, I gathered speed while crossing the barren athletic field. I was keenly aware of the logistics of making the motorcycle jump that I was about to attempt. From my previous jumping attempts from this same location, I knew from experience that it could be a somewhat tricky landing since the paved parking lot of the apartment complex was positioned a full eight feet lower than the surface level of the grassy athletic field. I also knew, though, that with just the correct amount of speed, my motorcycle would reach the edge of the athletic field, and then the momentum would launch me several feet up into the air. When done correctly, my bike and I would sail effortlessly for up to one hundred feet or more before landing with a spine-numbing force onto the parking lot pavement.

In a flash, my motorbike had crossed the field as I made one last mental note of the lack of activity that day all around the apartment complex. Seeing nothing, I rolled the throttle of the dashing bike ever further to really attempt a high, long jump.

Over the edge we flew, higher than I'd ever attempted before, when suddenly my blood ran icy cold as a car hidden beside a large van slowly backed out of a parking spot and directly into my path of decent. Although I'd never spotted a glimpse of her inside of her hidden car, I'd discovered later that she'd been sitting for a while inside of her car writing a letter to someone. At the unluckiest moment for me, she finished her task, started the engine of her car, and then proceeded to back out into my path of impending destruction.

My bike and I were already launched at high speed into midair with no chance to abort, to slow down, or to change direction when she backed out and into my path. I knew within an instant that I was about to come face-to-face with death even though I'd tried to do everything within my power to prevent something such as this unavoidable crash from occurring.

Flying at about fifty miles per hour, my entire body flexed into a knot of muscles as the looming midair crash with the car unfolded before my terrified eyes. While still in midair and with a force beyond description, my motorcycle smashed broadside into the left rear quarter panel of her car with such a blunt force that the rear bumper on her car flew cleanly off her vehicle. The motorcycle's smaller size and forward momentum was no match for the unyielding larger car. The motorbike literally went from a hurling speed of fifty miles per hour to an instantaneous dead stop as the front wheel exploded from the impact, and the strongly constructed steel front forks twisted like two pretzels made of soft bread dough.

Immediately upon impact, it is difficult to describe what thoughts were going through my mind. I was launched forward as though shot from a cannon up over the top of my motorcycle, up over the top of the car, and slingshot out into the paved parking lot nearly one hundred yards before sliding, scraping, and rolling to a complete stop.

I lay there in utter disbelief realizing that I'd just hit a car broadside at a shattering fifty mile per hour with my motorcycle, yet for some reason, I wasn't dead. By this time, the flustered woman had exited her car and had rushed to my side expecting to see me injured beyond description or perhaps dead or at the very least bleeding profusely.

Although I was severely stunned from the impact, she carefully aided me to my feet. She kept repeating repeatedly, "I'm so sorry. I backed out from behind that van with the big blind spot on my left side, and I simply didn't see you! I pray you didn't break anything or have any internal injuries."

I slowly stood up and began accessing my overall bodily damage. The first item I removed was the safety helmet from my head. I was shocked to observe that at some point while I came crashing down onto the pavement, my head had struck so hard that the helmet received a large crack, which ran down the entire helmet, yet somehow, I had sustained no head or neck injuries. Next, I looked down at the pant legs of my denim jeans only to find that my left pant leg was torn all the way from my ankle up to my hip as a result from my losing battle with the parking lot surface. Oddly, I felt no pain as I cautiously walked around, and somehow, I hadn't fractured even a single bone through it all. My heavy leather motorcycle jacket had done its job magnificently, because although deeply scarred and scraped, it had successfully prevented me from attaining even the slightest case of road rash.

I don't know if it was the woman whose car I'd smashed into or it was me who was more shocked at my noticeably absent injuries after such a traumatic collision.

She breathed a slow sigh of relief then loosened up a bit when she joked, "You must go to the right church because that crash would have killed anyone else for sure!"

I smiled weakly at her, but I didn't have the heart to inform her that I was becoming all too familiar with my perpetual encounters facing death.

We exchanged contact information, after which I helped her load her damaged rear car bumper into her car, and then she departed. With more than a little effort, I hoisted my fractured and disabled motorcycle into the upright position then pushed, dragged, and pulled it to its resting spot near my bedroom window.

After rising from bed the next morning, I was so thankful to have had the weekend off from working or attending college. It took everything in my power to rise from bed.

I staggered to my bathroom mirror and noted that much of my body was covered front and rear with swollen dark bruises. I nearly fainted as I pressed my fingers into the muscles of my arms, my neck, my chest, my back, and my legs. I was literally unable to find one muscle group on my entire body that wasn't aching from intense pain. It was at that moment that I realized what trauma my body had dealt with just a few hours earlier.

Just prior to making impact with the car, my body and all my muscles instinctively tightened in reflexive anticipation for the impact. Then the collision resulted in me being thrust off the motorcycle where I landed with a tremendous force upon the pavement. No wonder then why every muscle within my body went on to ache for days to come.

In time, my miraculously minor aches ceased. Before long, and following the repair of my damaged motorcycle, I was once again riding my two-wheeler as though nothing had ever occurred. More than ever, I came to appreciate the absolute enjoyment of the feeling of the wind blowing upon my face again.

Some folks will never understand the reasons why others of us are drawn to ride motorcycles. I can sum it up with this cute antidote: "Motorcycle riders are the only people on earth that fully understand why a dog always sticks its head out of the window of a speeding car with an expression of sheer delight upon their face!"

Looking back, I feel so blessed that the woman who backed into my path was uninjured. Certainly, I realize and accept that, somehow, I was protected by an angel once again.

The final unanswered question that one may ask, though, is how did my father ever respond regarding this incident where I could easily have died while on my motorcycle? Did my father quip "I told you so"?

The answer is that he never knew about any of what had happened, but in either his lifetime or following his death, my father will ultimately know the truth. I'm afraid that even though a few decades have elapsed since my first motorcycle accident, he will hardly be able to contain himself about lecturing me. I can hear it now with all the intensity he can muster, "You crazy idiots that operate those death machines!"

CHAPTER 3

Death Wish on a Motorcycle

Growing up as a teenager of the outlandish 1970s, my view of the world in general was inadvertently modified and somewhat tainted. The '70s came blasting into my life just as much of the youth in America shifted their lifestyles toward longer hairstyles, bell-bottom pants, loud rock music, and watching crazy television shows.

One television show that left an indelible mark on me was called *The Dukes of Hazzard*. Seldom would I miss an episode of watching Bo and Luke Duke outwit, outsmart, and outdrive Roscoe P. Coltrain who was the inept Hazzard County deputy sheriff always trying to catch the Duke cousins doing something wrong. Each week I watched in fascination as Bo and Luke Duke in their awesome orange Dodge Charger muscle car named the "General Lee" would outrun the law enforcement time and again. The radical vehicular stunts amazed me as countless scenes showed cars jumping over barriers or leaping across canyons then speeding away only to leave the cops in the dust each time.

Watching *The Dukes of Hazzard* show each week began imprinting a dangerous thought in my mind at an impressionable young age. Although much of the antics on the television screen were obviously contrived and nothing other than television fantasy, it still somehow planted some precarious notions within my mind during each passing week. My mind was so imprinted that even years after *The*

Dukes of Hazzard television series was no longer on television, I still aspired to one day be like the Dukes and leave the cops in the dust.

From the time I received my drivers' license at sixteen years of age until my twenty-fourth birthday, I suffered numerous vehicular speeding infractions. In fact, I averaged between two and three speeding tickets per year during that short nine-year span of time. In all, I received twenty-five speeding and moving violations before I even reached my twenty-fifth year of life. Absurd as it may seem, I loved to drive fast and loved the feel of a powerful engine gathering speed as I guided various cars, pickup trucks, or motorcycles down the road at my command. Over time, it even became a lighthearted joke as I would reiterate to my friends about how I'd seen the interior car design of every model year of Highway Patrol car for the past nine years; all while sitting in a patrol car receiving yet another speeding ticket.

Living in Minnesota, the moving violations ruling was such that a driver was allowed up to three moving violations within any given calendar year. On the fourth moving violation, however, then one earned the privilege of standing before a traffic court judge who would decide whether to suspend the driving privileges of the guilty party. Twice during that nine-year period of my life, after earning my fourth speeding ticket within the same calendar year, I stood before a judge while he demanded to know why I should not have my drivers' license suspended and until I could learn to obey the posted traffic speeds.

Although each court appearance was unsettling for me, and even though I was severely reprimanded by the court, somehow, I never once lost my driving privileges. In retrospect, perhaps I should have lost my driver's license for a period, which might then have stifled my desire for speed and danger while operating a vehicle. The traffic fines I encountered were a mounting problem. With each moving violation I was cited for, the fines increased proportionately. So the first violation may have been a fine of $70, then the second violation may have been a fine of $150, then the third violation may have been a fine of $325, and by the fourth violation, the fine and consequences of losing one's driving privileges were enough to make even someone such as myself sit up and take notice of the pain and discomfort it could inflict on one's lifestyle.

With each driving violation, my parents would unleash a torrent of angry challenges onto me asking why I was so incapable of controlling my excessive driving habits. They were extremely upset as they would endlessly remind me that I was such an insurance risk, that it was becoming nearly impossible to find affordable auto insurance coverage for me. Although my mother and father never completely understood the underlying reason for my compulsion for speed was that I simply loved to go fast, and I loved to feel the unbridled power at my beckoning touch. That feeling is one which I'll probably never fully diminish, but as I've matured over the years, I've learned to control my insatiable desire for speed. This in and of itself has been a forced behavioral change since I no longer desire to pay such lofty fines to the traffic court systems or pay such exorbitant auto insurance premiums.

It is easy to imagine then as one analyzes my mindset and historical love of speed, why by the age of twenty-four and newly married, why I was destined to get myself into some real trouble before my new wife Astrid could even react.

****

In a previous chapter, I mentioned my love of motorcycles and how much I've always enjoyed the sense of freedom they provide as one seemingly flies down the road through the open air. One of my first married-life transactions involved trading my relatively small and very slow college motorcycle off for something more fitting for my desires.

For years, I'd been reading every motorcycling magazine I could lay my hands on. I'd become somewhat of an expert on every variation and design the motor-biking world had to offer. It had not gone unnoticed to me that in the late 1970s, Yamaha had designed and manufactured the fastest street legal motorcycle available for purchase. I had the "Yamaha 1100 Special" specs and test-drive reports all but memorized. That amazing machine boasted a lightning fast acceleration, and on the test track, it had logged speeds of 152 mph!

From the moment I read about that blazingly fast machine, I set my sights on owning one someday. In the back of my mind, one thought remained vividly clear. If I could somehow find a way to acquire such an unbelievably fast motorcycle, then I would never again have to deal with a speeding ticket from a law officer since there would be no way their cars could keep up. I foolishly believed that if the Duke boys on *The Dukes of Hazzard* could show up the cops then one day so would I.

Much to my new wife's dismay, shortly following our wedding day, I traded off my Honda 250 and paid a few thousand dollars to boot as I took possession of the fastest stock motorcycle in America at the time. The sleek, racy two-wheeled machine would take my breath away as it effortlessly accelerated to outlandish speeds with a mere twist of my wrist on the throttle. Never in my lifetime had I ridden a machine with such thrust and instant acceleration. From the moment I rode my new high-speed motorcycle away from the dealer, I believed I would never again be caught by a law officer desiring to cite me for a speeding violation.

It didn't take Astrid very long following our wedding to realize that she had married someone drawn to high-risk behavior unlike no one she'd ever witnessed before. On the day that I dialogued with her about my intentions to go skydiving, all she could do was stare blankly at me. Since I held a private pilot license, she had flown with me on a few occasions. As if that wasn't enough for her to absorb, she was now listening to me state matter-of-factly, "I've learned to fly an airplane, but now I want to learn to jump out of one!" In her way of reasoning, she couldn't figure out why any sensible person would even contemplate jumping out of a perfectly functioning airplane. For me, however, the palms of my hands got sweaty just from the sheer thoughts of such an exhilarating parachute jump from an airplane.

The stage was set, and my life was about to take an irreversible course that day many years ago. Astrid and I had made our first home together in central Minnesota, but the skydiving school I'd signed up for on that weekend was in southern Minnesota. I kissed my fearful wife good-bye and indicated to her that I'd see her safe and sound within a couple of days. With that, I threw a backpack on my shoulders with some extra clothes and some toiletries, put my full-face motorcycle helmet on, and then mounted my new motorcycle. My motorcycle was so new in fact that it had less than one hundred miles on the odometer, and I was carrying the license and registration application in my pocket since the actual license plate for the motorcycle had not yet arrived in the mail.

I could almost sense the taste of adrenaline in my mouth of what was to come as I left our driveway and sped off down the highway with the fading view of my new wife disappearing in my rearview mirror.

A few hours later, I'd arrived at my destination and was participating in the classroom instruction portion of the skydiving training. In our training, we learned about the physics involved in parachuting from an airplane. We were taught what to do if our main chute failed to open and how to properly deploy our reserve chute. We were trained how to jump from the plane then we were instructed on the proper procedure for landing. In all, due to the dangers involved, we spent several hours of skydiving classroom instruction before we were then legally able to jump from an airplane and with our own parachute deployed. I must say the classroom portion became very monotonous and repetitive; however, I would admit that one doesn't want to discover that you don't know what to do in an emergency when you are free-falling through the sky at up to 130 mph.

At long last, our skydiving classroom instruction came to an end. My six classmates and I were suited up, and our parachutes were attached. Next, we hopped into a powerful airplane modified for skydiving jumps, and within moments, we were climbing to an altitude one mile above the earth. Once we reached our jumping altitude, our instructor asked for someone to be the first to jump from the plane and indicated that it was always the hardest to jump first, but whoever does so seems to help the other novices gather courage to also make their jumps. I didn't hesitate even for a moment as I raised my hand to volunteer to perform the lead jump. Not surprisingly, no one else wanted to go first.

Since I'd flown an airplane several times, I'd seen the view of the earth many times from such a high altitude, but it is almost indescribable what a feeling it is to force one's legs to take a leap of faith from an airplane with the hopes the parachute will open without incident. My skydiving leap went flawlessly, and the rush of adrenaline provided a flush of excitement such as I'd never experienced before. I'll never forget my feelings of invincibility as I floated nearly one mile back safely to the ground.

To say that I was on a "high" following my successful leap from an airplane would have been a massive under-statement. At that moment, I remember having the sensation that I was almost indestructible and was beyond being able to die. I literally felt as if I could walk through a wall of fire and go unscathed. With such disproportionate thoughts, one can only imagine the trouble I was about to face on my motorcycle journey back home.

I departed the skydiving airport parking lot on my motor-cycle with thoughts of making it back home in record-breaking time since I had the fastest stock motorcycle in America between my legs. I was traveling on a stretch of highway that had a steady, steep incline up out of a river valley that climbed for several miles. I was riding my motorcycle at about the posted speed limit, when my motorcycle and I quickly came upon a big truck struggling to maintain speed up the steep incline. Without even a moment's hesitation, I twisted the throttle on my motorcycle built purely for speed and dashed around the truck in an instant. Within that instant, I'd been traveling at about 55 mph, and with only the slightest twist of my wrist, the motor bike rocketed up to over 90 mph as I raced past the truck.

Much to my dismay, just as I pulled back into my lane of traffic, a State Highway Patrol Trooper came over the top of the hill toward me. Whatever my speed was now that his radar detected me, I can assure you that it was well over the posted speed limit. As the trooper's car passed by, he hit his sirens and flashers. At that precise moment, I thought to myself, *If the Dukes can do it, so can I.*

Just as I rounded the top of the hill that the state trooper had just come over, I cracked my throttle again. Due to the twists and curves in the road, I limited my speed to about 125 mph. I kept nervously glancing back in my rearview mirrors, and since I never saw a patrol car ensuing, after a couple of miles of travel I eased back off my throttle. I was feeling a strong sense of satisfaction that I'd made the correct decision to purchase a motorcycle that couldn't be caught by a police car.

I was settling back into my motorcycle seat and relaxing when I viewed a most frightening image in my rearview mirror. It was a very angry State Highway Patrol Trooper pushing his 440-cubic-inch, four-barreled carburetor, specially equipped "Police Interceptor" squad car for every mile per hour it could muster. Those "Police Interceptors" in the day could achieve speeds of up to 135 mph.

I simply cannot describe my fright at seeing the oncoming police car and hearing his roaring engine appearing to prepare to hit me from the rear. By instinct, I twisted the throttle once again, but by this time, the road had straightened out and I gave the motorcycle all the throttle could take. Since my motorcycle had no windshield for protection, I'll never forget the unbelievable force of the wind pushing back on my body, as the speedometer leapt up to 135 mph, then continued climbing to 140 mph, then 145 mph, and finally hovered at 148 mph.

It was everything I could do to hold on to the racing machine. It almost felt as though I were doing pull-ups on the handlebars, simply trying to hang on at such breakneck speeds. Slowly but surely, the 13 mph faster travel of speed allowed me to pull away from the ensuing state trooper.

For a brief moment, my mind drifted back to *The Dukes of Hazzard* television show as I thought to myself, *I've finally made it a reality*. The actual reality of the matter, however, is a fast motorcycle speeding at 148 mph may be able to outrun even the fastest "Police Interceptor" squad car traveling at 135 mph, but no matter how fast a motorcycle can travel, it can't outrun a police radio! The speed of sound is 767 mph, so I didn't stand a chance!

Traveling at a speed of 148 mph, I was shocked at how fast a mile would click over on my odometer and in moments our high-speed chase had elapsed several miles. As I came to the outskirts of a rural town, I became suddenly aware of a mass of police cars converging on me from every direction. At that moment, I surmised that from a law enforcement officer's perspective, this is what may have been transmitted over their police radios.

"Trooper 243 is requesting emergency backup assistance. In high-speed pursuit of an un-licensed, red-colored motorcycle that may be stolen. Motorcycle driver is wearing a full-face helmet and is presently unidentifiable. Due to the suspicious nature of the chase, there is reason to believe the motorcycle operator may be transporting illegal contraband as well in the backpack being worn."

As I quickly came to the outskirts of the small town, my vision scanned an unbelievable scene. The police radios were certainly working overtime because I had one squad car immediately behind me coming from an easterly direction, I saw two more squad cars racing toward me from the west, I saw another squad car blazing in my direction coming from the north on different road, and lastly, I spotted the local town police squad car heading out of town toward me coming from the south. At that point with a total of five police cars chasing me, I suddenly felt hopelessness such as never before. My brain struggled with what to do next.

One side of me said, "Stop immediately and surrender before you die." The other side of me was driven by fear and spurred onward by adrenaline. I was convinced that trying to surrender only to plead sheer stupidity with the angry law officers might prove extremely risky at best. I literally feared for the beating I felt I might be in for if I tried to stop.

Without much time to weigh my choices, I decided it would be better to die trying to escape rather than be beaten by an army of angry cops. With that, I locked the brakes on my speeding motorcycle as I whisked up to the edges of the small town. I turned off the main highway and directed my machine into the heart of the rural town. There were several squad cars in hot pursuit with their sirens blaring and their lights flashing as I picked up speed on my way through the town. Luckily, there were no pedestrians in sight as I blasted through the small town. By the time I'd reached the other side of the town, my speedometer read more than 130 mph. With five police cars in chase, I literally leaped over the town's railroad tracks, and at 130 mph, the high-speed jump through the air would have made the Duke boys proud. The trouble was, the Duke boys were merely Hollywood contrived fictitious characters, and I was in a real struggle for life.

As I sped away from the town heading south, I once again pushed the upper speed limits of my motorcycle. After only a couple of miles, I suddenly realized that there were now two additional law officer squad cars coming from the south and heading in my direction. Once again, I locked up the brakes of my large motorcycle and maneuvered the machine down a dangerous rural gravel road. Racing motorcycles such as mine were never built for rural gravel roads, but I had become desperate to find a path of escape.

I raced over a hill traveling at over 90 mph when suddenly I found myself trapped. What I'd thought was a rural gravel road was a long gravel driveway leading into a dairy farmer's yard. I'll never forget the look of terror on the eyes of the farmer and his wife as they were crossing their yard making their way to their barn to milk the cows. They stopped dead in their tracks as I sped into their yard followed by two squad cars in pursuit. As I entered their farmyard, adrenaline must have given me superhuman strength as I spun my heavy motorcycle around as though it were a mere bicycle then raced on past the two police squad cars that had suddenly entrapped each other in the farmer's yard.

Out of the farmer's driveway, I raced once again as I made a mental note of the treacherous barbed-wire fences near both edges of long gravel driveway. As I once again crested the top of the hill leading away from the farm, my speed was more than 90 mph. My next view was almost too much to comprehend. Only a mere one hundred yards ahead of me were two state trooper squad cars forming a V-shaped roadblock. There was only a three-foot section of space between the squad cars where both troopers stood facing me with their handguns drawn and aimed directly at me. At that instant, I believed that one way or another I was going to die. I instantly reasoned that I had three choices I could make, and I had to decide without even a split second to contemplate my options. Choice one would have been to lock up my brakes at 90 mph on a dangerous gravel driveway, only to crash since the motorcycle could never have made a stop in such a short distance. Choice two would have been to try to slow down as much as possible and, at the last moment, veer off and crash into the treacherously jagged barbed-wire fencing. Choice three and the option I opted for was to maintain my speed, and then hope I could make it through the small three foot spacing between the squad car roadblock, praying the officers would not actually shoot me.

It all happened so fast that comprehending the next chain of events is unsettling to me. Once the troopers realized I was unable to stop my motorcycle in the short distance before encountering their squad cars, they jumped away from the opening they'd been posting in front of. The memory is seared into my mind as one of the troopers shouted, "Stop or I'll shoot." Since I was unable to physically stop my motorcycle, I surmised that I was indeed about to die and perhaps the time had come when my Lord felt enough was enough with this rampant human being. The trooper's .357 Magnum pistol made a deafening crack not once, but twice, as I dashed past the officer. Suddenly, I started losing control of my motorcycle as my mind raced to decipher why was I doing this and had I simply gone mad. At first, I wondered if I'd been shot, thinking that perhaps I was so amped up on raw adrenaline that possibly I couldn't even feel the bullet enter my body. My next thought was that perhaps one of my motorcycle tires had been shot out, which is why I was losing control.

As it all played out that day, neither had happened. I was somehow miraculously unscathed by two close shots from a deadly handgun. My tires were somehow miraculously intact. I had simply hit a patch of loose gravel and nearly dumped the motorcycle as a result.

As I came to the end of the driveway, the rest of the squad cars were pulled into the driveway along one side of the drive. My sense was that they had parked their squad cars fully expecting the fleeing motorcyclist to be apprehended by the first four squad cars committed to the farm driveway. I hit the road leading back into the small rural town going north, and in an instant, I was again at the top end of the speedometer reading. I made a quick glance back over my shoulder and couldn't believe my eyes. There was a total of seven law officer squad cars involved in chasing me down, but because of the nature of the narrow and restricted farm driveway, each one of them were blocking each other's exit. I gained valuable time in my escape as they methodically worked to turn themselves around.

As I entered the town for the second time, I brought my speed down considerably. The first time I passed through during the high-speed chase, I hadn't spotted a single pedestrian. On my second pass back through the town, with all the commotion, with all the loud sirens, and with all the flashing lights, suddenly everyone in town had come out to see what was transpiring. The sidewalks on both sides of the street were literally lined with hundreds of citizens. I knew my battles with the police radio were still unfolding because up ahead the fire station had been summoned with a request to drive their longest fire truck out onto the main street of town in one last effort to stop or delay the criminal riding the rogue motorcycle.

I carefully slowed as I closed in on the huge fire truck blocking my escape. With everything that I'd encountered, at that point I could see no reason to run over or hurt the countless pedestrians who were lining the street. I quickly surmised the situation realizing that I couldn't make it around the fire truck on the right side. I also realized that there was no way to maneuver my motorcycle underneath the large truck. It did seem plausible, however, to inch my way around the back of the massive fire truck since there was a small space between the truck and the fire station door opening. I remember several firemen peeking around that corner wondering what to do. As I aimed the motorcycle for the space behind the truck, all the firemen scattered, leaving me with an easy path of escape.

Just as I reached the outskirts of the town once again and directed the motorcycle toward my final path of escape, I glanced back toward the town one last time only to view the firemen fervently trying to remove the large fire truck from the main street that was then blocking the path of the seven law officer squad cars who were back in full pursuit.

The delays in the town afforded me safe passage out of the area and when at last I reached home from that horrendous day, I had a lot to contemplate. On that day, I concluded that while it was possible to evade a ticket with a fast enough motorcycle along with some heightened riding skills, and with a whole lot of luck, it was apparent that it wasn't as easy as what my favorite television show had demonstrated. One would certainly think that a very strong lesson should have been learned that day as I nearly died trying to escape a simple speeding ticket. Did I learn my lesson? Well of course not!

With each passing week following my harrowing high speed motorcycle chase, my confidence grew, and my risk-taking behavior expanded. Sure, for the first couple of weeks following the incident, I laid low and took it easy regarding my driving tendencies. I knew, though, that there was little to fear regarding being discovered, because since my motorcycle was so new at the time, it had not had a license plate and because I had been wearing a full-face helmet during the chase, I was confident that there was simply no way of identifying me or the motorcycle.

As the summer progressed, I grew bolder. As I reflect on that year long ago, I realize now that the best situation for me would have been to get caught. Had I been caught, I would have dealt with the consequences and hopefully corrected my misguided behavior. As it turned out, though, I continued to push the limits and felt more invincible with each passing week.

It was late summer during the very same year. I'd ridden my motorcycle from my home in central Minnesota down to help my father and brother exhibit some of their Hereford cattle at the Iowa State Fair. Following the cattle show, I departed for the long drive back home. I was traveling on the Interstate Highway near Minneapolis. Although the flow of traffic at the time was traveling at more than the posted speed limits, I felt compelled to travel at an even higher rate of speed. I was very pleased with the amount of time I was saving as I darted my ultra-fast motorcycle in and out of the flow of cars. I was pleased that was until I rounded a bend of the highway and viewed a state trooper using radar to check vehicles for speeding.

As I passed by the trooper, he instantly flashed his lights, triggered his siren, and began pursuit. I must say that only an idiot like me in my state of mind would have made the decision to engage in a second high-speed motorcycle chase within the same summer. As I'd mentioned, however, reflecting, I believe the only way that I was going to cease my rampant behavior was to finally get caught or to die trying to escape.

My motorcycle was once again asked to perform at breakneck speeds as I dashed in and out of the flow of traffic, and at times, I would dash right between two cars or two semitrucks. Although I put some quick distance between the law officer and myself, he quickly found the fastest way to keep up with me was speeding along the outside shoulder of the highway. I decided that my best option of escape was to exit the Interstate Highway, so at the next exit, I sped onto the off-ramp and then quickly accelerated onto an adjoining highway.

Almost as though I were stuck in the same reoccurring nightmare, the police radios started encircling a noose ever tighter around my neck. As with my first chase a few months earlier, I had the speed and motorcycling driving skills to evade and outrun any immediate squad cars, but this time I couldn't seem to evade the incessant call of the police radios demanding more backup assistance for a high-speed chase.

I was keenly aware of at least four squad cars chasing me down through the traffic dense area when at last I locked my brakes and made a hard left turn down what appeared to be a back street. This decision was the beginning of my end. As I raced down the street in hopes of finding some opening in which to outmaneuver and ultimately escape the ensuing squad cars, I suddenly realized that I'd driven down a dead-end road leading to a community park and playground. It was déjà vu all over again as I reenacted nearly the same scenario as I'd driven down the dead-end farmer's driveway only a few months earlier.

Envision me coming upon this hidden park at a high speed of travel followed by five squad cars in hot pursuit. Since it was a warm, lazy Saturday afternoon, the park was overflowing with parents and their young children.

All at once a soccer ball came bouncing out onto the street followed by a young child chasing it down only about one hundred yards ahead of me. This was one of the most profound moments in my life as I made a split-second decision about what had to be done. The choice was actually very easy since I could've either continued with my current high-speed path only to run over an innocent child or chose to lock up my brakes, drop the motorcycle to the pavement, and pray for the best.

All these years later, I'm still haunted by the frozen look of fear on the child's face as I made eye contact with him. I did everything within my power to lock up the brakes on the motorcycle. My speed was too fast, however, and I lost control of the large motorbike. The motorcycle came crashing down onto its left side while crushing both my leg and ankle underneath. It seemed an eternity as the motorcycle continued to slide down the street in a shower of sparks toward the frozen little boy, only to come to a complete rest a few feet from the child.

SCOTT D. GOTTSCHALK

In a flash, there were police cars and police officers everywhere. I pulled myself out from underneath my severely damaged motorcycle somewhat relieved to still be alive and very thankful that I'd averted a collision with the small child. People from the park were quickly gathering around as the first of several law officers equipped with their billy clubs made their way to me as I sat in a daze upon the street next to my damaged motorcycle.

What I'm about to explain next is not easy to describe and was an unfortunate circumstance for all who were involved on that fateful day. What happened next was the very thing I'd always feared the most if caught following a high-speed chase. The officers involved in my chase were obviously amped up on their own adrenaline as they carried out their high-speed pursuit. Law officers are often asked to risk their safety in pursuit of criminals. Once they have a fleeing suspect contained, it can be all too easy to lose control of the situation.

Although I was still groggy from the impact of the motorcycle accident, I was all too aware of the angry law officers running toward me with their billy clubs poised to strike. I raised my hands in a sign of surrender and to emphasize that I was unarmed, only to be hit squarely in the middle of the face by the first law officer's billy club. The impact broke my nose and shattered my eyeglasses. As another officer arrived, I raised my right hand in defense hoping to avoid being hit again in the face, but the small baseball bat-like billy club connected with my right forefinger giving me a compound fracture of my finger. A third officer then began smashing me on the back with his billy club. I took such a beating on my back that it caused my entire back to turn black and blue a few hours later.

The three law officers continued to express their excessive anger toward me in the form of a billy club beating and doing so in front of a large group of pedestrian witnesses when at last a ranking law officer finally arrived at the scene and demanded his patrolmen cease their actions. I was so thankful to have the beating stop as I lay in street in my own ever-growing pool of blood. The actual motorcycle crash had been painful, but it paled in comparison to the beating the law officers had administered.

Everything from here out is a blur to me, but I know that I was handcuffed with my hands behind my back and then read my rights. Next, I was put into the back seat of a squad car in excruciating pain as I was forced to sit on my handcuffed hands including sitting on my right forefinger with a bone protruding through the skin. I was then transported to the local jail. It was at the jail that I was fingerprinted and then allowed to clean my wounds and eventually give my statement. I was asked several times if I wanted to be attended to by a doctor, but I refused the offer. I ended up spending the night in jail before being released by paying a bond to await my court appearance.

I arrived in court about one week later a very scared and very pitiful young man. In my heart, I felt the Lord had finally found a means to break me of my bad habit. No matter the beating I'd taken at the hands of the out-of-control law officers, in my mind I knew I'd been raised to take responsibility for my own actions, and I was prepared to do just that.

My wife, Astrid, drove me to the Hennepin County Courthouse that day and neither of us had any idea of what to expect. I signed in with the clerk of court, and then we waited for our court hearing. We waited for what seemed forever, and we worried about what the eventual outcome of my wayward activities would be.

At last, I was called before the judge. He asked me where my representing attorney was. I proclaimed that I was in court to plead guilty and to take responsibility for my actions. The judge sat quietly as he read my case file and surmised the beating I'd been given during my arrest, which was fully documented within the file.

He leaned over his bench and said, "I would strongly suggest that you obtain a lawyer who can review your case and guide you toward the proper plea." He went on to state, "If you can't afford an attorney, then the court will appoint one on your behalf." Lastly, he commented, "This is a pretrial hearing, so I'm recommending that you obtain the services of an attorney and properly prepare for your upcoming court case."

The judge looked down at me with total disbelief as I responded, "Your Honor, I've never done anything illegal in my life, except that I've incurred a few speeding tickets. This time I made a big mistake that I'm not proud of, but I've been raised by parents who instilled in me to always own up to one's mistakes and pay the price." I went on to say, "I respectfully decline your suggestion to obtain an attorney. I would like to request that rather than appearing back in court later, I would like to enter a guilty plea at this time and ask for your sentencing effective immediately."

One could hear a pin drop in that courtroom that day as the judge contemplated my request under such a unique set of circumstances.

At last, he looked down at me and asked, "Why did you do it when your history demonstrates that you are a decent, law-abiding young man?"

I shared, "I've always been drawn to speed, and this time I let it get the best of me. I would even have to admit that my fear of getting beat by law officers probably helped drive my illegal actions to flee."

The judge once again proclaimed, "In my opinion, I believe that the circumstances and harshness of your arrest, along with your clean record, warrants an attorney's representation on your behalf."

I responded with, "I appreciate your input, Judge, but I still plead guilty and request sentencing at this time."

With that, the judge stared me straight in the eye and went on a rant as he remarked, "Young man, as you stand before me, you are faced with a total of twelve misdemeanor counts, gross misdemeanor counts, and felony counts, the worst of which is a felony assault charge with a deadly weapon, namely using your motorcycle to potentially run down another person. In addition, you are faced with multiple violations of fleeing a police officer, resisting arrest, reckless driving, reckless endangerment, speeding more than 100 mph over the posted limit, failing to yield, failing to stop, crossing over the center line, passing in a none passing zone, failing to signal, and illegally passing on the highway shoulder."

I stood before the judge as though a statue as he briefly stopped his rant and sized me up.

Suddenly, he proclaimed, "It is the court's belief that your history reflects a decent, law-abiding background, yet it is apparent you have a propensity for speed, which eventually led to a severe lack of judgment on your behalf."

With that, the judge imposed his sentence upon me, and I was forever changed as a result.

The judge spoke again by stating, "You have pleaded guilty to the charges before you. It is my decision to drop all your charges, except for a gross misdemeanor charge of fleeing an officer of the law. As a result of your actions, I'm fining you fee of $1,000 payable today to the clerk of court. In addition, the court hereby sentences you to a one-year term in jail to be served immediately in the Hennepin County Workhouse."

I felt my knees go weak as the judge continued, "I'm electing to stay the final eleven months of your sentence, and you will earn your release upon good behavior after which time you've served thirty days of your sentence behind bars. Following your release from incarceration, you will meet with your parole officer to discuss your future direction."

I stood in stunned silence as the judge gathered his thoughts for one more proclamation.

As the judge pointed his gavel at me, he firmly stated, "Young man, I'm placing you on a lifetime probation, meaning if you ever so much as get the slightest moving violation while operating a motorcycle anytime during the rest of your life, the court reserves the right to incarcerate you to serve the remainder of your eleven-month sentence behind bars."

With that, he slammed his gavel and demanded the court bailiff to handcuff me and had me transported to the county jail.

As I was led from the courtroom in handcuffs, I looked back at my teary-eyed wife sitting alone in the courtroom and who was as unsure of what had just happened as I'd been.

****

That was a long time ago, but my life was and has been forever changed for the better because of that summer. I could go into detail about what it feels like to spend day after day behind bars in a cell so small one can reach out and touch the walls. Or I could make comments about quality of jail food or how one keeps their mind functioning properly with nothing but bars to stare at day after day. I could even delve into how challenging it is mixing with a general population of convicts, many of whom have made a lifetime career in the criminal element. I could make an entire chapter out of just this fraction of my life, but I'm not going to.

What I am going to do is mention the good that came from my experience. During my thirty days of incarceration, I had a lot of time to think about what kind of a man, what kind of a husband, and what kind of a person I wanted to be. Although by some standards, a thirty-day sentence behind bars is nothing compared to some jail and prison terms, I assure you it was plenty long enough to impact a change on me.

What a glorious day it was when my loving wife, Astrid, arrived to take me back home. I would never have believed I could miss anyone as much as I'd come to miss her. On our emotional drive back home, I promised to gain control of my compulsion for speed. To show my commitment to avoid any future jail time, I immediately sold my beloved motorcycle. I reasoned that it would only take one lapse of judgment where the power and acceleration of the speedy motorcycle might cause me to lose control, and I'd then be destined to spend the remaining eleven months of my sentence behind bars. I was so motivated by the judge's threat that it was nearly twenty years later that I finally purchased another motorcycle and began passionately albeit cautiously riding again. For the record, however, in the nearly thirty years of riding motorcycle once again, I've always been cautious about getting a moving violation while riding a motorcycle.

It seems like a lifetime ago that I had a death wish on a motorcycle. In one fateful summer, I was consumed by the power and speed provided me by a dangerously fast motorcycle. That along with my risk-taking personality combined for not one, but two exposures to certain death. Was it possible for someone as me to be only twenty-four years of age and still somehow survive death so many times?

A great deal of time has passed, and as a result, I've learned some important lessons in life because of that summer. Through all those trials and tribulations, I came to realize two infallible facts in my life. One fact was that my wife unconditionally loved me and was willing to stand by me through even the worst possible scenario. The second fact was that even with a death wish on a motorcycle, I hadn't been making good use of my existence.

CHAPTER 4

Grizzly Bears Not Biker-Friendly

We coined our guy foursome the "Wild-Hogs" as we departed on the motorcycle expedition of a lifetime attempting to ride our motorcycles an astounding ten thousand miles round trip over the course of eighteen days all the way from Minnesota to Alaska and then back again.

Maynard Moen, his cousin Jeff Moen, along with Maynard's brother-in-law Dennis Miller, and I had planned our extensive motorcycle journey for more than one year. Each of us had ridden together for several years, and we'd established a lofty goal of one day riding our motorcycles together within all fifty states within the USA along with motorcycling through every province of Canada. With our next cycling objective at hand, we'd studied several books whose subject matter was motorcycling in the wildernesses of northwestern Canada and Alaska, and we felt mentally and physically prepared for our trip in every way. Months earlier, we had mapped out an exacting route complete with motel reservations for each night's stop during our trip.

Our foursome group of extremely opinionated bikers was equally split regarding their preferred choice of motorcycle brand. Maynard and Dennis each proudly rode their large Honda "Gold Wing" touring motorcycles while Jeff and I with equal pride each rode our large Harley-Davidson "Ultra-Classic" touring motorcycles. The bantering and insults about whose brand of motorcycle was superior was ceaseless before, during, and following our Alaskan road trip. To hear our group throw insults at each other made casual observers wonder if we were friends at all, but our ultimate respect and appreciation for each other has never been in question.

At last, we set out on our trip wondering if our machines would mechanically hold up for such an endurance test. Our established route demanded that we average well over five hundred miles per day for eighteen days in a row. Along the way, we knew that we would endure extreme weather conditions including everything from snow to rain and temperature ranges from a frigid thirty degrees up to a steamy ninety degrees. Our road conditions were just as varied since we encountered everything from well-paved highways to dangerous rock roads to treacherous mud-covered stretches of road under construction.

As suggested by some of the books we'd studied about attempting such an excursion with motorcycles, each of us carried a spare gallon of fuel due to the lengthy distances between towns at times. Prior to setting out on our Alaskan motorcycle trip, each of us had our motorbikes serviced with new tires and engine tune-ups, but even so, Jeff and I each carried one spare motorcycle tire if we might encounter tire troubles while deep within the wilderness territories.

Another sound suggestion from one of the books we reviewed indicated that when riding a motorcycle through wilderness areas populated by bears, one should never pack food or sweets of any kind on the motorcycle or in one's clothing. The author cited a story of how he and a friend rode their motorcycles to Alaska. According to the story, his friend's Harley-Davidson motorcycle engine quit working many miles from civilization. Rather than leave his valuable motorcycle stranded along the highway and then ride tandem to the next town on the other bike, he opted rather to remain with his disabled motorcycle while his buddy drove off to seek help.

About two hours later, the buddy returned with a truck and was shocked by what he discovered. His friend's once beautiful motorcycle was strewn out along the highway laying in several fractured pieces while he clung for dear life to a branch high up in a nearby tree. As the truck neared the carnage, he crawled down from his perch in the tree and explained what had transpired.

Shortly following the departure of his friend to seek out assistance, a large grizzly bear had lumbered toward the man and his motorcycle. In fear for his life, the man had climbed as high into a nearby tree as possible. From his safe vantage point, he watched as the bear used his razor-sharp teeth and claws to shred his motorcycle into metal shrapnel seeking out the candy bars packed into the compartments of the motorbike. Even though the candy bars had been wrapped in their original packaging and although they were encased in sealed plastic sandwich bags, the grizzly bear's keen sense of smell and ravenous hunger drew it to the source. With little effort, the gargantuan bear ripped and tore the expensive motorcycle into irreparable pieces.

****

We began our ten-thousand-mile journey in a freezing rain with temperatures hovering near thirty degrees. Even so, our foursome was optimistic and raring to set out on our exploration adventure. The only items packed in any of our cycles consisted only of clothing and toiletry items. We had all mutually agreed that packing along any form of food or candy would be risky at best.

The miles flew by as we traveled scenic mile after mile through parts of the western United States, then parts of western Canada, and then we journeyed along the storied "Alcan Highway" through northwestern Canada in route to Alaska.

For the first several days, we traveled safely and trouble-free. We were spellbound by the awesome and rugged beauty of the geography we covered. Never had any of us experienced such breathtaking views of mountains, glaciers, lakes, and valleys. We were mesmerized by the quantity of wildlife we encountered along the way. By the halfway mark along our route, we had already seen fifty bears along with countless elk, moose, deer, mountain goats, and mountain sheep to name a few. In fact, the wildlife encounters on our trip at times posed a road hazard, as we had to be watchful to not hit some of the large animals as they often dwelled on or near the roadway.

Several thousand miles into our journey, it seemed that everything was all too perfect. Before long, I came to realize that my luck was about to run out, as I was about to experience one of the most challenging forty-eight-hour periods in my entire life. And yes, another close encounter with the Grim Reaper awaited me.

We discovered that our group's good luck ran out as we were about to depart from one of the many isolated gas stations deep within the Yukon territory of Canada. Jeff's Harley-Davidson motorcycle barely started as we prepared to continue our northerly course. With grave concern, Maynard, Dennis, and I walked over to try to determine the cause of Jeff's problems. After noting that his battery was losing charge on the voltage gauge, I instantly realized Jeff's motorcycle was probably in need of a new electronic stator and voltage regulator. Even though everything had gone so well over the course of the previous days of traveling, we knew the joyride was suddenly over.

We huddled together to determine our best course of action to take. It was obvious that Jeff's motorcycle battery was nearly drained, and since his electrical system was failing to charge his battery, we were all too aware that before too long his battery would fail to produce the necessary spark to ignite the engine. We were concerned with how to get his cycle to a Harley-Davidson motorcycle repair shop. Luckily, I'd packed along a book showing all the available repair shops on the American continent. Much to our dismay, the closest shop was nearly seven hundred miles away in the direction that we were traveling. Unfortunately, our best option was to backtrack one hundred and fifty miles to a repair shop in a town that we'd traveled through only hours earlier.

I called the shop to alert them that Jeff and I would be traveling together back to their location, and I requested that they remain open until we arrived to get the repairs completed and put our trip back on course. We all agreed that it made absolutely no sense for all four bikers to ride an extra three hundred mile round trip to get Jeff's motorcycle repaired. As a result, Maynard and Dennis departed with their Hondas on the original course, while Jeff and I ventured back toward the direction we'd earlier traveled on our Harleys. We were never in doubt about implementing the "buddy-system" while traveling in such extreme wilderness surroundings. If the books we had reviewed prior to our trip had taught us anything, was that it was a good idea to always travel with another biker if you or your machine has difficulties.

We waved goodbye to Maynard and Dennis, promising to meet up with them at our next motel stop many, many hours later.

Jeff and I had hoped that his motorcycle battery would provide enough spark to get us most or all the way back to the distant repair shop. Unfortunately, his bike killed for a final time only a few miles down the path. We sat there uncertain on what to do next. I volunteered to allow Jeff to ride with me in tandem on my motorcycle to try to locate a truck for hauling his disabled bike. Jeff asked that I go alone to seek out assistance while he waited by the side of the road with his expensive Harley-Davidson motorcycle. I expressed my concerns about leaving him stranded all alone in a bear-riddled wilderness while I left to seek help. I cited the example once again of the story in the book we'd read where a grizzly bear had destroyed a motorcycle trying to get at a candy bar. It was to no avail, as Jeff insisted that he would not leave his valuable motorcycle unattended alongside the road.

With that, I left in hopes of finding someone with a truck to transport Jeff's motorcycle to the repair shop before too much of the day had elapsed. As I once again traveled in a northerly direction putting on miles in the wrong direction, I prayed and hoped to find a solution to our dilemma. Several miles along my route, I came to a run-down pit stop along the side of the roadway. I inquired if there was anyone with a truck or a trailer that could transport my friend's motorcycle to a repair shop that was over one hundred miles away.

The man at the counter dialed a phone number and handed the receiver to me. Before long, I'd negotiated a hauling fee from the gentleman on the other end of the line. Within a half an hour, while riding my motorcycle, I led his ancient pickup truck in disrepair toward Jeff's position.

As we came upon the stranded motorcycle sitting alongside the road, Jeff was nowhere to be found, which left me with grave concern. I shouted out his name, and then I whistled loudly wondering where he could be. All at once I spotted Jeff nearly a half a mile away as he came out from the thick timber forest on the opposite side of the road from where his motorcycle sat.

He looked ghostly white as I inquired, "What on earth are you doing way down there away from your bike?"

Jeff replied, "I was waiting alongside my motorcycle when suddenly a big black bear came out of the woods walking toward me. I knew I wouldn't be able to climb a tree, so I hiked down the road about a half mile and hid in the trees."

I started laughing almost uncontrollably as I stated, "Jeff, if that big bear would have wanted to get you, then your hiding in the woods would not have done you much good."

Poor Jeff was so distraught over his bear encounter, I couldn't help but throw a jab at him when I retorted, "You know, Jeff, I'm glad I'm riding with you on this trip.

And starting from this moment on, I'm taking off my heavy, thick leather biker boots and putting on my lightweight tennis shoes instead."

Jeff asked, "Why would you do something stupid like that?"

I could no longer keep a straight face as I broke out laughing and said, "If a big, mean, man-eating grizzly bear decides to attack us I'm going to be able to run away."

With a questioning look on his face, Jeff said, "You can't outrun a charging grizzly bear because they can outrun a running horse for short distances!"

With a look of total seriousness, I remarked, "Jeff, I'm not going to try to outrun the grizzly bear. I only want to outrun you when he starts to chase us!"

I don't know if Jeff ever forgave me for those comments, but it sure gives me a chuckle when I think about it.

With all the drama behind us, we were at last able to load the crippled motorcycle on the rickety truck and transported it to the waiting repair shop. Although we arrived at closing time, the motorcycle mechanic remained on duty until Jeff's bike was completely roadworthy once again. Jeff paid the cost of his repairs, thanked them for their service, and we readied ourselves for our long journey to catch back up with Maynard and Dennis. The time was 6:30 p.m., and we had nearly four hundred miles to retrace before our extended day could close.

Just as we were about to leave the motorcycle repair shop, the mechanic remarked that the rear tire on my motorcycle looked low. Not giving it too much concern, I asked if I could borrow the air hose to fill my tire up to the proper level. Having done so, Jeff and I scurried off without any further ado.

It was well past midnight when Jeff and I arrived at the motel where Maynard and Dennis were impatiently awaiting our arrival. Tired though we were, our group of four "Wild Hogs" lay awake and laughed until we cried as we shared the stories of the trying day.

The following morning, we awoke refreshed, ate a hearty breakfast, and were ready to do battle with the wilderness once more. That is until I walked up to my motorcycle and noted that my rear time was entirely flat. With the help of my biker friends, we pushed my motorcycle over to an available air hose and filled the tire back to the proper inflation. Next, I rode my bike into a water puddle in the parking lot to determine where the leak in the tire was. It didn't take long to determine that sometime during the previous day's escapades in my efforts to help Jeff, I'd somehow run over a nail or some other sharp object, which subsequently put a large, deep puncture in my nearly new rear tire. The air simply bubbled and gushed from the hole as we once again questioned what to do with another disabled motorcycle.

By this point in time, the two Honda motorcycle riders were chirping like jubilant birds about how it appeared that we would never complete our journey to Alaska since the Harley-Davidson motorcycles were always in need of some sort of repairs. All I can say is "ouch," but I've always noted that what goes around sooner or later it comes around. Sure, the Hondas performed spectacularly during our lengthy journey on this trip, but the time came on other trips where the repair needs landed squarely on the opposite brand of motorcycle.

I scratched my head while looking at my leaky rear tire wondering what to do. I knew that replacing the rear tire on a Harley motorcycle requires some special tools and specific adjustments from a certified Harley-Davidson repair shop. Once again, I drew my book out to determine where the closest repair shop was along our chosen pathway. Much to my dismay, the closest shop was the one that had repaired Jeff's motorcycle just the day before. That shop was now four hundred miles in the wrong direction so an eight-hundred-mile round trip to replace my rear tire was out of the question. The only other choice was to try to find a way to limp my motorcycle on a bad rear tire nearly one thousand miles to the next certified repair shop.

Traveling such a long distance and through such wilderness conditions on a faulty rear motorcycle tire is an unsafe predicament to be sure, yet I had few acceptable options. I contemplated the idea of finding someone who could haul my motorcycle the excessive distance, but I determined that idea to be simply cost-prohibitive, much less difficult to secure someone to make such a long haul anyway.

Risky though it was, I made the decision to overfill my rear tire at every fuel stop along the way, which worked out to be on intervals of about every two or three hours, and then ride on with our group wasting no time as we tried to reach the next pit stop to reinflate my tire. A normal rear tire should be inflated to forty pounds of pressure, but over the course of the next two five-hundred-mile days, I overinflated the tire to sixty-five pounds of tire pressure. The tire spewed out its air so rapidly that I learned to fill it up at the last moment before we departed from a fuel stop. Then as we traveled along the oftentimes poor road conditions, my rear tire pressure would fall ever lower with each passing mile. Many times, in the final fifty miles, it would be rather difficult to operate the motorcycle with the rear tire so spongy and soft. Each time for each fill for the entire two days, my rear tire would fall from the sixty-five pounds of tire pressure down to only ten or fifteen pounds of pressure. I worried if my tire would even hold together until we reached the distant repair shop. With each passing mile, I feared a worst-case scenario of my tire blowing out and losing control of my motorcycle.

Thankfully, the tire held together all the way through the two-day ordeal, and ultimately, I reached the repair shop. Having called ahead a day earlier, I was the first repair job scheduled for that morning.

Maynard, Dennis, Jeff, and I were lying on the grass alongside the repair shop as we waited for my tire replacement. I felt terrible putting our entire group behind schedule since we were faced with a seven-hundred-mile journey awaiting our departure.

At last, I remarked, "There is no reason for all of us to sit around here for an hour or two as we wait for my tire repair. I'd prefer that the three of you take off without me. You can take your time and even do some sightseeing along the way. As soon as my bike is finished, I'll take off. And since I'll be traveling by myself, I should be able to make up some lost time. My guess is that before the end of the day, I'll catch up to the three of you, and we can ride the rest of the way to our evening motel stop."

Maynard came back with, "No way. We already know what can happen when we leave someone in our group to fend for themself in this wilderness country. Trust me, and I speak for our entire group, when I say that we don't mind waiting until everyone is ready to depart."

I retorted, "Guys, I appreciate your concerns, but I'd rather you go on ahead without me. It will be fun to travel much faster by myself as I attempt to catch up to you. Anyway, I'm sure nothing is going to happen once my motorcycle tire gets replaced."

Famous last words because YES something was going to happen!

My three buddies mounted their motorcycles and waved as they departed from the parking lot of the repair shop. Deep down inside, I was happy to see them go since I knew that they would enjoy their leisurely day of riding together without dealing with the stress of when my repair work would be completed or how late we would arrive at the motel. Truth be told, I was looking forward with anticipation at bringing up the rear all by myself as I attempted to catch up to our group.

Nearly two hours following the departure of my riding friends, my motorcycle was equipped with a new rear tire, and I was ready to journey forth. The sky was a beautiful shade of blue with only a few cotton-ball-like clouds dotting the sunny sky. I savored each deep breath that filled my lungs and relished in the woodsy organic smells of the uncivilized wilderness area.

I was sixty miles away from the town where the repair shop had been located. As I twisted the throttle ever higher for more speed, a smile crossed my face as I thought about how lucky I was to be able to experience God's wonderful wilderness creation. For nearly one hour, I had not seen another vehicle or met another human being of any kind. My exuberance became uncontrollable as I began singing out loud while cascading down the highway at full speed. It dawned on me that at my current rate of speed, I would have little difficulty in catching up to the guys in my party. How wrong can one be?

All at once, my motorcycle engine backfired with a deafening bang, as my motor stopped running altogether. I dare say I was very concerned since the past few days had been filled with one mechanical challenge after another for either Jeff or me. Without the engine operating, my bike and I silently coasted to a stop alongside the shoulder of the roadway. I had not seen a single vehicle for more than one hour nor had I traveled past any signs of human inhabitation. The dense virgin forest encroached upon the road on both sides for as far as the eye could view, which left me extremely nervous about my isolation.

When I tried to restart my motorcycle, I was astonished to realize that there was no electronics anywhere on my bike. All my gauges were dead, I had no lights, and when I turned on the ignition switch, I was met with an absolute deafening silence. I carefully scoured every portion of the motorcycle looking for any reason for the electronic failure. Seeing none, I felt my heart rate elevate as I considered my scant options.

It was a long shot, but I turned on my cell phone only to discover that the screen flashed a "No Service" reading.

Much earlier in our journey, our biker group had discovered that in the extreme wilderness areas cell phone coverage was nonexistent. Panic started creeping into my thoughts as I pondered what to do.

I was alone in an isolated grizzly-bear-infested area with a totally disabled motorcycle, with no cell phone coverage, and without any human encounters. My thoughts spiraled downward as I tried to determine what course to take. I knew that waiting idly along the side of the road was not a good option since roads such as the one I was stranded on seldom had motorists passing by. With the real risk posed from being hunted down by a grizzly bear, I realized that I was not only a "sitting duck" if I stayed, but also risked becoming a tasty grizzly morsel of food if I tried walking in either direction for help. The thought of walking seemed outlandish anyway since I knew the nearest town was sixty miles in the rear, and the nearest pit stop traveling forward was over seventy-five miles away.

In moments such as those, I find comfort and strength in prayer. Whatever the outcome, my experience reflects that God comes to my aide if only I will be humble enough to ask.

I sat upon my crippled motorcycle, folded my hands, bowed my head, and then prayed, "Heavenly Father, I try to direct most of my prayers toward thanking you for all of my many blessings. I've always felt it improper to pray too often for things that I'm in need of. Truth is Lord, this time I'm in a bit of a fix and I'm asking for your help and guidance to show me the way out of this dilemma."

Just as I closed my prayer by whispering, "Amen," my ears instantaneously picked up the faintest sound of a distant vehicle coming from my rear. I looked skyward and shouted, "Thank you, God!"

At first, I couldn't understand why the distant truck was taking so long to approach me. From my vantage point, it appeared that the truck would drive a short distance and then stop while one or two men would walk to the back of the truck. It appeared that they might never reach me; so at last, I left my stranded motorcycle and started trekking back toward the remote truck. It suddenly dawned on me that they were some kind of road-repair crew patching potholes in the road. I picked up my walking pace when I began to fear that they might finish their road repair work on that distant stretch of road, and then suddenly might turn around and drive back to the town sixty miles away. I knew that I had to contact them before it was too late or face a far worse fate.

The men hopped in their truck for one last time and prepared to do a U-turn on the highway to depart in the opposite direction when they spotted me far out in the distance hurriedly rushing toward them while waving my arms high in the air. I let out a sigh of relief when I observed the truck stop in the middle of the U-turn and then drive in my direction.

The two Native American Indian men drove up alongside me and asked what I was doing. I shared my dilemma and indicated that I either needed to locate a landline phone to call someone for help or else I needed to find someone with a truck to haul my motorcycle back sixty miles once again to the same repair shop that I'd departed from a few hours earlier. I inquired if there was any way that they could haul my motorcycle in the back of their truck, but since it was nearly full of hot, smelly asphalt for road repairs, that choice was deemed out of the question.

Standing on the road and leaning into one of the truck's open windows, I asked the two of them for any help which they could provide. They indicated that there were no landline phones anywhere in the region, and they stated the obvious when they reminded me that there was no cell phone service either. Next, they indicated that there was a small Native American Indian encampment ten miles ahead, but they felt there would be little chance of anyone being present during that time of the day.

I pleaded with them to transport me to the encampment so that I could at least try to locate someone who could assist me. The two men were not too thrilled about the idea of making a twenty-mile round-trip journey in the wrong direction, but after offering to reward them with something for their services, I was soon squeezed between the two inside their rustic highway repair truck.

Before long, we entered the obscure encampment, and as the men had predicted, I knocked on door after door to no avail. It appeared the entire encampment was merely a ghost town. After knocking on ten different dwellings, I walked up to the final two feeling defeated and dejected. As I knocked on the door, I was surprised to hear a dog viciously barking. Next, I heard an elderly man's voice shout at the dog to be still, as I watched the door open ever so slightly.

The man peered through the crack in the door and asked, "Who are you, and what do you want?"

I responded by saying, "I was traveling toward Alaska on my motorcycle, but about ten miles back everything stopped working. Would you happen to have access to a pickup truck or trailer, and if so, could I pay you to haul my bike and me back to the cycle repair shop seventy miles from here?"

The old Native American Indian proclaimed, "Yes, I have a pickup truck. And yes, I could haul you. And yes, it will cost you two hundred dollars cold cash!"

My prayers had been answered or so I thought now. I requested the services of the two road repairmen for a while longer to travel back to my stranded motorcycle and then assist with loading the heavy machine onto the pickup truck. They agreed, and in a short while, the four of us were attempting to load the eight-hundred-pound motorcycle onto the bed of the pickup truck.

The elderly gentlemen drove his truck down into the ditch and then positioned it so his open tailgate faced the shoulder of the road. We then placed a semirotted two-by-six-inch board spanning it across the shoulder of the road onto the tailgate of the pickup truck. We determined that the best way to guide the heavy motorcycle onto the narrow board and into the waiting pickup truck was for me to straddle the cycle and steer while the three men pushed from the rear.

That was a near-fatal choice on my behalf because as I guided the motorcycle wheels across the creaking boards, it suddenly dawned on me that it would never support the nearly one thousand pounds of total weight amassed by the motorcycle and me. Before I could react and try to stop them, the three men pushed even harder on the bike. As I'd feared, the weight was too great, and the near-rotten board splintered into pieces. Tragically, I was dislodged from the motorcycle and fell several feet to the ground just as the eight-hundred-pound machine crashed down on top of my rib cage with a thunderous impact.

My vision nearly dimmed as I struggled to remain conscious. For what seemed like forever, I made a futile effort to breathe since the impact not only knocked the wind out of me, but the brunt force also severely fractured three of my ribs. In addition, the falling motorcycle badly bruised my left hip and leg.

The startled men came instantly to my rescue by hoisting the heavy machine off my injured body. As I gasped for breath while lying dazed in the ditch, the three men somehow found a way to load the motorcycle and get it strapped down. I thanked and paid the two road repairmen, and then the elderly man and I made our trek back toward the repair shop.

The pain in my rib cage from that bumpy, harsh, one-hour long ride goes beyond description. My ribs were so injured that I could move several of them around with my fingers. The pain was so intense that I was only able to endure short, shallow breaths.

Eventually, we arrived back at the repair shop and unloaded the motorcycle. I sincerely thanked then paid the man for his merciful help, and then watched as he drove away.

The mechanic who had replaced the rear tire of my motorcycle earlier in the day was quite shocked to see me back again and in such an injured condition besides. I explained exactly what had happened to the machine and to me. Before long, he proposed a theory to me on what he thought to be the electrical source of my predicament. He speculated that perhaps the thousands of miles that I'd logged on rough roads over the past several days had somehow loosened the electrical wires connected to my motorcycle battery. He showed me how the loose connection had started to create a burning electrical arc, which then in turn caused the main electrical circuit breaker for the motorcycle to fail, thus killing all of my electrical functions on the motorcycle.

The good news was that he discovered what he theorized was the problem and then fixed it. The bad news was that he couldn't positively verify for certain that he had in fact determined the root cause of the problem. He cautioned me that since the motorcycle was now started and running that I should consider keeping it continuously running until I reached my final destination for the night. He suggested it might be a good idea to only shut off my engine once again when I had the security of being with my riding partners once again. I agreed with his recommendations, but I knew that it would be difficult at best to fill up my motorcycle fuel tank while leaving the machine running and vibrating.

It was time once more to try to try to head in the direction of my three motorcycling friends, only this time I was far less confident that I could reach them at all. The logistics didn't bode well for my travels of that day since Maynard, Dennis, and Jeff had all left the repair shop earlier in the day at 9:00 a.m. I'd left the shop for the first time about 11:00 a.m. following my tire replacement. Now because of all my difficulties, I was departing for a second time at 3:00 p.m., a full six hours behind my buddies. To make matters even worse, I was faced with a daunting seven-hundred-mile route through desolate wilderness traveling all by my lonesome with broken ribs and a bruised hip and leg. As if it could be any worse, I had little confidence that my motorcycle would even keep functioning since the mechanic had instructed me to keep it running in the event the electrical problem had not actually been solved.

Before I left the safety of the repair shop and the town, I used their landline phone to call ahead to the motel that we were all supposed to be staying at on that night. I provided the desk clerk with all the details, and then requested that she pass along the information to the rest of my biker group once they arrived. With that, I swallowed several aspirin to dull the pain coursing through my body and then I ventured back out into the wilderness once more hoping to survive what had become a most grueling and excruciating motorcycle ride.

The miles on my motorcycle odometer started clicking by one after another. With my rib, leg, and hip injuries, my pain threshold was peaked higher than I could ever remember. Surely with the extent of my injuries an endurance ride on a motorcycle would not be what a doctor would have prescribed for me. Obviously, bed rest was not a viable option, but on a positive note, by enduring so much pain, I was able to keep from falling asleep from utter exhaustion throughout the seemingly endless hours and miles.

I literally held my breath as I approached the exact spot in the road sixty miles from the town and the repair shop. I gave a silent prayer of thanks as my motorcycle appeared to be contentedly rumbling along its pathway past the troubled spot. Seventy-five miles farther, I pulled into my first fuel stop. As instructed, I left the motorcycle idling as I filled the vibrating machine's fuel tank with gasoline.

The fuel stop attendant came outside and shouted, "Hey, you, don't you know it is illegal to put gasoline in a tank with the engine running? You could cause an explosion or start a fire."

I responded back with, "Yes, I know, but I'm having electrical problems with my motorcycle, and I've got to keep it running or risk not being able to get it started again."

The disgruntled attendant threw his hand in the air then spun around and went back inside. I ran inside as soon as I'd finished putting fuel into the motorbike, paid the man, then hurried along on my way once again.

I repeated this process while riding the several hundred miles through the wilderness. Late afternoon had long since become early evening, and eventually, the clock was nearing the middle of the night. I made one final fuel stop about 11:00 p.m. I distinctly remember feeling three sensations. The first was how exhausted I'd become riding in total isolation for so many hours. The second was how much pain was coursing through my body as the endless hours of motorcycling was jarring every nerve within my injured body. Third, I realized that throughout the daytime and evening hours, I'd forgotten to consume any food. Tired, injured, and hungry wasn't a happy place to be in, but I knew if I could endure another two or three hours of riding, I would finally reach the final motel destination situated near the Alaskan and Canadian borders.

With my motorcycle still idling outside, I purchased a cold sandwich and a bag of M&M's candies. I was so hungry that I nearly inhaled the sandwich while walking back toward my motorcycle. I decided to pack my bag of candy into one of the compartments of my bike and intended to eat the candy later down the road. This was a near-fatal error in judgment because I knew better than to pack candy while traveling through grizzly territory.

I didn't think I would ever make it, but according to my calculations, I only had about fifty miles to go. I found it rather strange that since I was so far north, it wasn't all that dark considering it was nearly 1:00 a.m. While speeding down the forlorn highway, I found it strangely comforting that *the land of the midnight sun* provided me a safer pathway of travel throughout the nighttime hours.

I lamented over the fact that I had been driving through that wilderness for over seven hours without seeing another vehicle on the road. I was so thankful, however, because even though I hadn't shut down my motorcycle engine for nearly ten hours straight, it was a fitting relief to know that it continued to bring me ever closer to my destination. I felt some euphoria with each passing mile knowing that within an hour, my endurance test would soon be over.

Perhaps the Lord had just one more test in mind for me though.

Through the 1:00 a.m. twilight din of the sky, I detected a troublesome thunderstorm rolling across the mountain region that I was driving through. Up ahead, the vigorous storm clouds were spewing lightning and thunder, and I could see the trails of a heavy rain flowing from the ominous clouds. It suddenly dawned on me that my rain gear was packed away deep inside the compartments of my motorcycle. After such a harrowing day and night of travel, I couldn't envision being able to endure much more torture from a cold, soaking rain.

My first instincts were to simply ride through the downpour of rain though since I was a mere fifty miles from the end of my route. I determined that it would simply be better to get wet and ride on rather than to take the time to stop and suit up in my painful condition. My initial decision was quickly altered as the pouring rain suddenly turned into marble-sized hail falling from the sky. In an instant, I stopped the motorcycle on the very center of the highway. The hailstones stung like bullets as I gingerly got off my motorcycle. By this time of the night, my broken ribs were screaming in agony, and I was incapable of moving too fast because of the pain.

As I prepared to locate my rain suit, I realized that I would need to shut off the engine of my motorcycle to first locate the rain gear and then find a way to cautiously get into it with my severely injured ribs, hip, and leg. Had I not been in the middle of a hailstorm, I most like would have reconsidered my choice, but with little time to contemplate,

I shut down my motorcycle for the first time in more than ten hours.

The machine no sooner came to a silent rest when the hail ceased falling and the thunderous downpour slowed to a mild rain. I determined that since the motorcycle was shut down and since it was still raining, my best option would be to continue with getting into the rainsuit. I winced in pain as I raised my tender left leg and inserted it ever so slowly into the pant leg of the rain gear. With my leg halfway into the rainsuit, it suddenly dawned on me just how eerie and quiet everything around me appeared. As I surveyed my surroundings, I suddenly felt the sensation of the hair on the back of my neck starting to prickle. I sensed danger, but from what or from where?

I looked back down the highway from which I'd come and saw nothing out of the ordinary. Next, I investigated both sides of the dense virgin timber nearly encroaching upon the highway. Still, I saw nothing out of the ordinary, but why were my senses on high alert? Why was I sensing a strange sense of danger and paranoia?

As I glanced down the narrowing highway tunneled between the mountains and dense forest, I suddenly became keenly aware of my serious problem. My eyes strained and then focused on a gigantic grizzly bear that had emerged from the timber. The grizzly was about seventy-five yards from me, and it appeared that he was simply crossing the road up ahead of me. But then he stopped, raised his nose high into the air, and sniffed so loudly that I could hear him. As soon as I spotted the bear, I hadn't moved a muscle, but with his keen sense of smell, he suddenly turned directly toward me.

For what seemed like an eternity, the grizzly stared in my direction, and I stood motionless staring back with my left leg stuck inside the pant leg of my rainsuit. The standoff between man and beast canvassed enough time that I was fraught with worry. It suddenly had dawned on me that the grizzly bear was trying to pick up not only my human scent, but he was most likely drawing on the sweet aroma of my hidden package of candies. My mind raced with thoughts of how to survive such an emerging crisis.

I devised two separate plans and readied myself to implement first one and then the other if my first plan failed. My first plan demanded that if the bear moved in my direction, then I would reach forward with my right hand to start my obstinate motorcycle hoping and praying that my failing electrical system would in fact fire the engine back to life. My intent should the motorcycle fire was to then mount it as quickly as humanly possible considering my rib and leg injuries then blast on out of the impending danger.

My secondary options were dismal at best under the circumstances of my motorcycle failing to fire. I knew I couldn't outrun the grizzly, and I was quite sure that I would be unable to climb into a nearby tree due the severity of my injuries. For those reasons, I devised the only plausible means of escape I could think of at the time. Should the motorcycle fail to fire, I intended to quickly reach for my M&M's candies, rip open the package, and then start dropping one candy at a time onto the ground while slowly walking backwards. Even though my left leg was tangled inside the pant leg of my rainsuit, I deducted that perhaps the bear would be so intent on slowly eating one piece of candy at a time that he would ignore my retreat. Well, okay, I'll admit it now, this was not a very plausible scheme, but with a man-eating grizzly facing you, one's mind can only hope that the killer bear can be manipulated by his sweet-tooth craving.

As the bear stopped in the center of the road only yards from me, then sniffed the air, then turned to face me, I was simultaneously devising my two separate plans of escape. The total elapsed time was only seconds before the bear began walking toward me. My fear elevated and my entire body was suddenly covered with in a cold, clammy sweat. I could taste the strange metallic sensation of fear inside my mouth as I reached for the starter of my motorcycle as the grizzly bear advanced.

Once again, I prayed, "Lord, please let this motorcycle start. This is not exactly the way I want to die."

In all my life, I've never been so happy to hear a motor fire up as I was at the instant my Harley-Davidson engine sprang back life. I twisted the throttle allowing the ear-shattering exhaust pipes to fill the air with a most welcome roar. The oncoming grizzly bear was so startled that without haste he spun around and dove back into the dense timber.

I wasted little time in getting myself into the remainder of my rainsuit and then I sped off down the dark trail toward my destination. As soon as I was up to speed, I cracked open my package of M&M's candies and relished in the fact that I was eating them rather than the grizzly eating either my candy or me.

****

By 1:30 a.m., I finally made it into the small town where the motel was located. I was met on the outside edge of the town by my worried riding partners—Maynard, Dennis, and Jeff along with two law officers. They had all feared the worst and had all gathered to form a search party. Their intent was to backtrack in hopes of locating me since I was late in my predicted arrival, and no one had received word of my whereabouts.

Everyone was mystified as I recanted my tale of mechanical troubles, injuries, and subsequent grizzly bear confrontation. It was only after telling of my encounter with the grizzly bear that the motel clerk shared some alarming information.

The clerk described another motorcyclist's encounter with a grizzly bear in nearly the same location as my confrontation only a couple of weeks earlier. We all listened in suspense as she told of how the biker had not turned up one evening. The following day, law officers were sent to search for him. About fifty miles back and in about the same area as my grizzly bear visit, they found the biker's motorcycle parked alongside the roadway. The officers shouted out his name without a response. Shortly thereafter, while walking along the road ditch next to the forest, the biker's helmet was discovered lying in the ditch. When the officer stooped to pick up the helmet, the man's severed head was discovered still inside the helmet!

Further investigation determined that a large grizzly had decapitated the man with a single powerful blow from one of its enormous paws and further blood-trail evidence proved that the grizzly bear dragged the body off into the timber. The body has never been recovered, and it was assumed that the grizzly devoured him.

We sat in stunned silence at hearing such a gruesome tale of another biker's demise in nearly the same location as where I'd encountered the mammoth grizzly bear.

I didn't sleep much at all that night even though I was thoroughly exhausted. Between the pain from my injuries and the haunting thoughts of what my grizzly encounter may have become, sleep escaped me.

The following day, I placed a call back home to inform Astrid of just how treacherous my previous day had been. She listened to every detail with grave silence. When I had finished, she asked me to hand the phone over to my friend Maynard. Although I thought it to be an odd request, I called Maynard over and indicated that my wife wanted to speak directly with him.

Maynard grasped the phone and said, "Hello, Astrid. What can I do for you?"

My dear, sweet wife who takes such pride in her quiet and calm demeanor, without a moment's hesitation shouted into the phone, "Maynard Moen, if you ever let my husband out of your sight again on one of these biker guy trips to God only knows where, I'm going to find you and tan your hide. From this point forward, I don't want you to let Scott out of your sight even if he goes into the bathroom. Is that understood?"

Maynard responded, "Yes, Astrid. I understand."

****

Over the eighteen days of our round-trip motorcycle journey to Alaska and back, we experienced countless wonders of our Lord's wilderness creation. We all survived the rigors of the trip and gained the experiences of a lifetime.

For whatever reasons, the Lord challenged me with several tests during a forty-eight-hour period. Through it all, I suffered from injury, from pain, from defeat, and from unbridled fear. As the events of those trying hours unfolded my faith was certainly tested, and it was battered, yet my prayers were always answered.

CHAPTER 5

Motorcycle Devastation

It is with my deepest humility that led me to share this narrative. Without doubt, this specific story had such a personal life-changing impact that I was inspired to share an essence of the many saving graces throughout my lifetime within the pages of my second book, *Nine Lives to Eternity*. As I reillustrate the events that afflicted me in the next few pages of this book, they have often been described by others as nothing short of miraculous. The saga of my near-death experience following such a catastrophic accident allowed me to bear witness to the wonders of the Lord and of his boundless mercy, grace, and love for his wounded and fallen children.

The subsequent account, which I'll share, ultimately answered an important question that I've always pondered. Why does the Lord allow my life to continue, and does God have some unfulfilled mission for me yet to complete? During my lifetime, I've invested heavy deliberation trying to resolve what God's purpose for me really is. The following recount is a description of what brought me nearer to death.

I've been granted a God-given blessing enabling me to communicate through written words. Such words of faith have allowed me to fulfill a portion of what I believe is my mission to our Creator. This is my personal witness and testimony to the vast wonders of our Lord.

SCOTT D. GOTTSCHALK

****

Motorcycling has been one of my greatest passions as formerly mentioned throughout this book. I can think of few activities in my lifetime that granted me such an exhilarating feeling of freedom. Anyone who has ever ridden a motorbike can attest to the thrill that can be derived by simply twisting the throttle and then surging forward with unbridled power and speed. The unobstructed view while riding a motorcycle is like none other.

For more than fifty years of my adult life, I've owned and operated a motorcycle of one form or another. While there are countless high-quality motorcycle brands on the open market, my preference has been to own and ride the iconic American-made Harley-Davidson motorcycles. I've always loved throwing a leg over the seat and then settling down into the recesses of the machine, literally becoming one with it. Sometimes comparisons have been made that *one sits up on* other brands of motorcycles, but *one sits down on* a Harley. I've always been capable of riding immense distances on my Harley because it is arguably the most comfortable machine that I've ever driven even though I've ridden or owned many other brands.

I've constantly been able to log many more miles within any twenty-four-hour period on my motorcycle than in any other type of car or pickup truck that I've ever operated. For nearly a decade, I've annually logged between fifteen thousand and twenty-five thousand miles per year on a motorcycle. Those kinds of miles may seem implausible to some but imagine if you will that I reside in the wintery state of Minnesota where the motorcycle riding season is oftentimes only three or four months in duration.

Other bikers that see my motorcycle during any given riding season will often ask whether I ever wash my bike. They are usually taken aback by what twenty thousand miles of road grime and bug guts adhered to the motorcycle looks like. For the record, I only clean and wash my motorcycle one time each year always at the end of the riding season. I'd much rather be riding than cleaning, and I've always chuckled how many motorcycle owners seemingly invest more time washing and polishing their machines than riding them. In today's modern fad-induced motorcycling cultures, there are countless owners that appear to haul their motorcycles around the country on a trailer more often than riding their machines.

Living in Minnesota, I'm often asked how I can log so many miles per year with such a challenging environment. I respond by saying warm clothes and good rain gear is worth their weight in gold. I also note that a "fair-weather" biker or a "weekend warrior" biker never seems to log too many miles. On the other hand, during our short Minnesota riding season, I try to ride my motorcycle every chance I can despite the inclement weather conditions. When I can, I try to ride my motorcycle for work-related activities as well as utilizing it for a couple of extensive motorcycling vacation trips each year.

The foursome biker riding buddies I described in the previous chapter would qualify as "hard-core" motorcycle enthusiasts by most definitions. Over the years, Maynard Moen, Jeff Moen, Dennis Miller, and I have canvassed America with our motorcycles. Those cherished friends would do most anything and everything for one another. Our "Wild Hog" group of guys have ridden motorcycles thousands and thousands of miles together covering all fifty states in the USA, all the road-accessible provinces of Canada, and even ridden our motorized two-wheelers in Mexico. Each year, we enjoy a lengthy motorcycle ride together that varies in distance from four thousand miles up to ten thousand miles. Our annual trip together is oftentimes in the beginning of the summer and results in only a fraction of the total miles each of us rides throughout any given biking season.

SCOTT D. GOTTSCHALK

****

The annual trip we planned for the summer was intended to be divided into two separate portions. For this year's ride, Jeff was unable to participate so our foursome became a triad. The first portion of the route involved Maynard, Dennis, and I riding our motorcycles all throughout the eastern provinces of Canada as well as riding through the New England States in the northeastern sector of the USA. The second portion of our ride called for Maynard and Dennis to then continue together in tandem on their pathway toward their homes in Minnesota while I branched off to attempt a solo cross-country endurance ride.

During the first portion of our route, we had spectacular weather with only a few challenges. Partway through our journey, we did have to invest some time at a Honda repair shop to replace the flat rear tire on Dennis's motorcycle. I must add that I took immense glee in laying it on thick with poor Dennis about what an irritation it caused that his Honda repairs were delaying our scheduled travels.

Maynard also had a harrowing near miss when he almost hit a deer. I was riding in the very rear of our group with Maynard just in front of me and Dennis leading our group. We were riding along at 10:00 a.m. and driving at the posted speed of sixty miles per hour when a deer bolted from the thick trees alongside the highway and rushed directly at Maynard's motorcycle. From my observation point, I was spellbound as the deer somehow timed its leap perfectly and literally jumped over the top of Maynard's windshield and then ran away unhindered. At the next pit stop, we dialogued what a close call Maynard had with the deer. If I remember correctly, Maynard indicated that he probably needed to change his underwear because of his deer encounter. We all agreed that a direct hit with the deer traveling at such a speed would have resulted in a tragic scene for sure. None of us were aware that it had provided a sinister premonition of things to come.

At last, our wanton travels brought us to the state of Connecticut after we'd ridden together in excess of three thousand miles. The time had finally arrived to implement the second portion of our intended route. Maynard, Dennis, and I enjoyed one final evening meal together as we swapped tall tales and played jokes on each other. At last, we prepared to check into our motel rooms. We gave each other goodbye hugs since Maynard and Dennis would be departing together on their separate destination and at a different time than my departure the following morning.

As I said my final goodbye to my dear friends on that evening, I had no idea that I might never see either of my biker brothers again.

I started my cross-country motorcycle endurance ride early the following morning. As a certified member of a long-distance motorcycle association, I'd already successfully completed several endurance rides over the years, so I knew my capabilities. Within the ranks of this association are tens of thousands of motorcycle enthusiasts that enjoy the personal challenge of riding vast distances on their machines under quantifiable circumstances. Anyone who achieves their certification subsequently earns a bumper sticker that proudly displays they are the toughest bikers on the planet. Let it be perfectly clear, none of these endurance rides is a race but rather is a ride that can only be sanctioned if safe, legal motorcycle practices are implemented.

The endurance ride certification that I sought called for riding from one coastline of America to the opposite coastline. Furthermore, I customized my route to attempt to ride my motorcycle from ocean to ocean within forty-eight hours. It is no stretch of the imagination to understand why it is considered one of the most difficult of all the endurance ride certifications to attain. For this ride, a biker had to secure two verifiable witnesses who document the time, the date, the address, and record the motorcycle odometer reading for both the start of the ride and then have two additional witnesses secured to verify the completion of the ride.

The ride has always been considered an "extreme ride" because of the demands it places on both the rider and the machine. Since so few have ever successfully completed a certified coastline to coastline ride, I'd been dreaming of attempting the endeavor for years. Although one can choose several different routes, all of which have varied mileages, I chose the longest and most difficult course for my certification attempt. My mindset has always been to go "BIG" or don't go at all!

Doing the extreme ride within the forty-eight-hour itinerary that I decided upon posed an extremely difficult option, but I've always subscribed to the philosophy of "No pain, then no gain." Some would say that the criteria, which I established for my ride, was pure insanity. The objectives that I set for my ride were to begin the time clock for the ride by pulling a symbolic sample of water from the Atlantic Ocean on the beaches of Connecticut. My chosen route was to then drive through the entire midsection of the nation on Interstate Highway 80 across the entire United States. My intent was to log the more than three-thousand-mile distance and then complete the ride by drawing a symbolic sample of water from the Pacific Ocean in California.

There was little room for error and for most the task appeared insurmountable. I relished in the challenge since I'm capable of functioning quite well on little if no sleep for days at a time. I'd done the calculations and the sheer challenge of trying to average sixty-five miles per hour for forty-eight hours straight without a break really got my competitive juices flowing, but the concept put fear into all who knew what I intended to attempt. The key takeaway though is that participants in a ride such as this are not allowed to break the posted speed limits, and their ride is not certified if the ride is not performed in a lawful manner.

An important motto of our elite group of long-distance motorcycle riders comes from the quote, "We should never go beyond our mental and physical limitations and that it is better to accept failure so we may live to ride another day."

Before starting this ride, my father had called me and shared, "Scott, you are one of the only people I know that takes delight in doing what any normal person on this planet would consider pure, unadulterated torture."

After getting the signatures from my two starting witnesses, I garnered my cherished sample of Atlantic Ocean seawater and then mounted my big Harley for the greatest endurance ride at that point in my lifetime. Mile after mile and hour after hour, I maneuvered my motorcycle westward through state after state. The endless series of road construction hurdles combined with heavy traffic near the large metropolitan areas kept me frustrated to be sure.

As my certification time clock ticked past the first twenty-four-hour benchmark, I'd logged in excess of fifteen hundred miles without a single incident. I was overjoyed to have ridden through the most densely populated portions of the nation while remaining slightly ahead of schedule. By the halfway point, I was so pumped to reach my target that I felt little if any fatigue even though I'd been operating the motorcycle nonstop for an entire twenty-four-hour time frame without stopping for a rest of any sort.

With each passing mile into the more sparsely populated regions of the western states, my spirits rose as I drew nearer to my goal. By that point, I was ever so slowly getting ahead of schedule since the posted interstate highway speed limits in most of those states was a blistering seventy-five miles per hour. With the miles on my odometer rapidly increasing, I had little doubt that I would become one of only a handful of intense long-distance motorcycle riders to attain the lofty goal of crossing the United State at its widest point and from ocean to ocean within forty-eight hours on my motorcycle.

At 9:00 p.m., on the second night of travel somewhere in the state of Wyoming, I made a call to my wife Astrid for the first time during the thirty-six hours that I'd been on the road. I said, "High, honey, I can't talk long since I've got to get back on the road. I wanted to let you know that I've logged over two thousand miles thus far, and I'm still on pace to reach my endurance distance target. I just must drive all night for a second straight night and then I'll call you about 8:00 a.m. from the Golden Gate Bridge in San Francisco, California. Please give our sons, Trevor and Travis, an update on my progress so they won't worry. I love you, and I'll call you in the morning when I've reached my target."

My wife, Astrid, stirred uneasily in a fitful slumber as the night came and then went. She rose with the morning dawn and impatiently waited for my 8:00 a.m. call. She watched with nervous anticipation as the hands on the clock first moved past the 8:00 a.m. mark and then moved past the 9:00 a.m. mark and then past the 10:00 a.m. mark and still she waited for the promised call from her fanatical husband. Her intuition and instincts sensed that something was dreadfully wrong, but what? She knew that if I could have, I would have called by 8:00 a.m. no matter if I'd reached my target or not, so why wasn't I calling her?

****

I hung up the phone after talking with my wife evermore inspired to accomplish my long-distance motorcycling goal. As I roared out of the truck stop and onto the highway, I felt invincible knowing that I had less than one thousand miles left to reach my final mark. My thoughts drifted to how wonderful it would feel to take off my heavy motorcycle riding boots and socks and then let the warm, soothing California beach sand seep in between my bare toes when finally my long ride would terminate.

I was still making amazing time as I entered the state of Utah. At about 1:00 a.m., I stopped at a truck stop to fuel up near the Utah and Nevada borders. Throughout my cross-country journey, I'd been intermittently wearing my motorcycle helmet. Prior to my departure, I'd documented which states required motorcycle helmet usage and which ones had no helmet laws. I'm a strong advocate of freedom of choice rights when it comes to motorcycle helmets. I believe that under certain accident circumstances, a helmet may provide some protection, but I also feel that under certain accident circumstances, a helmet may in fact cause critical neck injuries or possibly even contribute toward death. The bottom line is that I don't believe that all our freedoms and rights should be legislated and mandated. Whether you are a motorcycle rider who wears a helmet or one who chooses to ride without a helmet, the simple fact is that most motorcycle crashes can be so horrific that a helmet can only provide minimal protection for saving the life of the biker.

Throughout my cross-country journey, I wore my helmet whenever it was mandated by state law and then I rode without a helmet while in any states that allowed the freedom of choice. Even the most ardent helmet-wearing motorcycle enthusiast would find it difficult to wear a heavy, hot helmet continuously for forty-eight straight hours. At 1:00 a.m., I strapped my helmet onto my head, knowing that I would shortly be entering into the helmet-mandated state of Nevada. In retrospect, I was glad that I chose that moment to wear my helmet.

For the next hour, I traveled in dark isolation at the posted speed limit of seventy-five miles per hour. As I crossed over the border into the desolate stretches of Nevada, I made a mental note of how few vehicles were traveling during that time of the night. The moon remained hidden, so everything around me was ominously black except for the shallow illumination of my headlight piercing into the night. I wondered to myself what the scenery might look like had it been daylight. Dark though it was, I could vaguely detect that I was traveling through a desert area of some kind because of all the large sagebrush thickets encroaching along the four-lane interstate highway.

I looked at the illuminated clock on the dash of my motorcycle, and it read 2:00 a.m. I quickly did the calculations in my head and took satisfaction in the fact that I'd logged more than twenty-five hundred miles by operating my motorcycle nonstop for an amazing forty hours straight. I let out an immense sigh of satisfaction as I realized that I was still well within my targeted schedule. I was looking forward to covering the remaining five hundred miles within the allotted eight-hour time frame so I could finally bring a close to my arduous endurance test.

The cruise control of my motorcycle was locked in at the posted seventy-five miles per hour. I was the only soul on the highway. Suddenly, my soul was in the grasp of the Lord.

The final memory I have from that night and one which changed my life forever focused upon the collision of my motorcycle with a substantial mule deer that had just darted into my path. I didn't even have time to say a prayer before the carnage began.

****

The Nevada State Highway Patrol accident report outlined the frightening facts. The large deer had appeared so suddenly in my pathway that I hadn't had time to hit the brakes on the motorcycle. The cruise control on the obliterated bike was hauntingly still locked in at seventy-five miles per hour. The accident report indicated that the collision with the deer sent the motorcycle and I careening toward the right-hand shoulder and ditch of Interstate Highway 80 at a deadly high rate of speed. Based on the tire tracks lodged into the sand of the ditch, it appeared that I'd fought with the rampant machine trying to direct its course of travel back onto the highway. In my failed attempt to correct the doomed course of travel, the right-side foot peg of the motorcycle struck the thick wooden trunk of a large sagebrush plant. The momentum and mass of the motorcycle cleanly severed the thick bush near its base as though a hot knife slicing though butter. Consequently, the motorcycle flipped end over end a total of three times crashing to a battered stop one hundred and sixty feet out into the sagebrush dense desert. The accident report further described the measurements of each of the three separate and distinct divots left in the sand by the hurling motorcycle. With each horrific flip, the motorcycle left shattered wreckage strewn along the entire pathway of the accident.

It was 2:00 a.m. I was alone, I was unconscious, I was severely injured, I was nearly dead, and my fate lay with God. My fractured body lay alongside the annihilated motorcycle where I'd been catapulted far from the highway into the dark and eerie desert wasteland. No other vehicles had witnessed my accident, and no one traveling along the road would be able to detect my hidden plight. My body and my soul were truly in the hands of the Lord as my fragile fate was yet to be determined.

Four and a half hours later at 6:30 a.m., I was still undiscovered and still unconscious. How much longer could I possibly live with such extensive injuries while lying in such a hostile environment?

Out of nowhere, a mystical, out-of-focus stranger bent over my body and with his face only inches from mine shouted, "HEY, ARE YOU ALIVE?"

Perhaps I was already at heaven's gates, but suddenly, I was startled out the deepest recesses of unconsciousness as my eyes opened.

As my eyelids fluttered, the stranger responded with, "You are alive."

At that moment, I had no concept of where I was nor did I have any recall of the collision that had occurred nearly five hours earlier. I found it extremely difficult to utter my words because I'd been lying unconscious for many hours with my mouth open. All throughout the night, mosquitoes by the hundreds crawled inside my mouth and throat inflicting their vampire-like damage.

I nearly choked as I spit out a dozen bloodsucking insects from inside my mouth. With my mind in a deep fog and while suffering from a swollen tongue and throat, I croaked, "Where am I?"

The stranger softly spoke, saying, "You are lying in a desert in Nevada."

"Why?" I replied.

The man soothingly uttered, "You've had a terrible motorcycle accident. Hundreds of other vehicles have been continuously driving past you at this very location for perhaps hours."

In my battered state, it was difficult for me to comprehend anything the stranger was sharing as I listened in silence. The man continued saying, "It's a miracle that you survived such a horrendous crash because there sure isn't much left of your motorcycle." I was instantly all too aware of how badly I was injured as I made a failed attempt to roll onto my left side. My attempts to roll onto my right side and then to try to sit up were also met with dismal failure. The pain coursing throughout my entire body was beyond words as I became gravely concerned by my inability to move.

I dejectedly realized that I couldn't move or sit up. Was I paralyzed? And yet, I could move my feet and wiggle my toes, but the pain from trying to move was unbearable.

The mystery man seemingly vanished as miraculously as he'd appeared. I mercifully lapsed back into deep unconsciousness again.

Thump thump thump thump thump was the deafening sound emitted from the emergency medical air evacuation helicopter as it prepared to make an emergency landing on Nevada Interstate Highway 80. Unbeknown to me, state highway patrol officers had shut down the flow of traffic on the major highway thoroughfare, enabling the rescue helicopter and its emergency medical team to come to my aide.

I was unaware of how long I'd been unconscious as I drew ever closer to death, but the earsplitting reverberations of the spinning helicopter blades shocked me back into consciousness for a second brief moment. The truth is that somewhere deep in the recesses of my mind I could hear a strange and distant thunder as the helicopter prepared to land, but as I reopened my glazed eyes, I once again had no concept of where I was or why I was laying in such pain amongst the sagebrush on the floor of a desert.

Within moments from the time that I detected the booming sound of the helicopter, almost instantly there were four emergency medical technicians working in unison to stabilize me and attempt to save my life. I have the foggiest recall of one technician readying a stretcher to transport me. A second technician used a large scissors to first cut the strap on my helmet, and then carefully remove it. The technician made note of the excessive gouges and scratches on the helmet, realizing that for this accident, it had performed its duty admirably. Next, he used his shears to cut through the sleeves and the front side of my thick leather motorcycle riding jacket, and then he continued to cut through and remove all my clothing leaving me only in my underwear. A third technician worked feverishly to carefully place head and neck restraints on me to prevent possible paralysis. The fourth technician inserted an IV needle deep into one of my veins and began administering some form of fluids and medication.

The last words I heard before everything went totally black again came from the technician just as he finished cutting through the front of my leather jacket. With grave concern, he said to the IV technician, "Oh boy, this guy has ripped his arm and left shoulder completely out of the shoulder socket and his dislocated appendage is dangling across the top of his chest."

I don't know if the shock of those words sent my mind back into the abyss or perhaps the IV technician injected a sedative into my vein to ensure that I wouldn't have to deal with any more pain for a few hours.

7:00 a.m. The helicopter lifted off with a critically injured patient en route for the Elko Nevada Regional Medical Care Unit located twenty-five miles away and located just to the east of the city of Reno. The hundreds of backed-up vehicles on the blocked interstate highway resume their travels once more wondering what poor soul required such an extreme medical air evacuation.

10:00 a.m. Astrid received a most terrifying call from the intensive care unit of the Elko hospital.

The nurse stated, "Hello, I'm calling from the ICU at our hospital in Elko, Nevada. Are you Scott Gottschalk's wife?

With bated breath, Astrid replied, "Yes, I am. Please don't tell me that my husband is dead!"

The nurse said, "I'm sorry to inform you that sometime during the middle of the night your husband suffered a catastrophic motorcycle collision with a deer. Unfortunately, he wasn't discovered or air-evacuated from the scene of the accident for nearly five hours, so his medical condition is very unstable. He arrived by helicopter to our emergency care facility, and currently, he is having emergency surgery in the operating room to try to save his life. He is currently listed in critical condition."

Astrid was so stunned that she could barely speak. She had wondered and waited for several hours for the promised call from her husband once he'd reached the shores of the Pacific Ocean, but rather she bore the shattering news of her mate's demise.

Astrid asked, "Do you know what happened and what his injuries are?"

The nurse replied, "I'm sorry, but I don't know any of the details of the accident, however I can tell you that he has been sedated since being airlifted to our facility. As soon as he arrived, we completed a CAT scan trying to determine if he had brain damage then an MRI was performed on his badly damaged left shoulder injury, and finally, we completed nearly fifty X-rays of his body. Finding all of his fractures was almost as though looking for a "needle in a haystack," but so far, we've determined that your spouse has fractured dozens of bones including fracturing his back in three separate locations." He has also fractured every rib in his ribcage.

Astrid felt her knees weaken, and the color drain from her face as the atrocious commentary registered in her mind. She remained in stunned silence as the nurse promised to contact her with more information as updated details became available.

11:00 a.m. My eyes slowly opened with my mind dulled from a deeper mental fog than I could ever remember. I was unaware that I was regaining consciousness following my major lifesaving emergency surgery. The total elapsed time from the moment of impact at 2:00 a.m. until 11:00 a.m. was an astonishing duration of nine hours. Except for two brief moments of semiconsciousness at the accident scene, I'd been unconscious for an extremely long time. But, hallelujah, I was alive!

As the haze began to clear from my mind, the doctor assigned to my case strolled into the surgical recovery room and leaned toward my face.

He spoke softly and said, "Mr. Gottschalk, I'm the doctor who has been working to save your life for the past several hours. I just want to mention that you are perhaps one of the most fortunate motorcycle accident victims anyone in this emergency medical facility has ever witnessed. I can assure you that we are never required to work on a biker who has crashed at seventy-five miles per hour because their limp and lifeless bodies are typically transported immediately to the morgue for the deceased."

As I stared deeply into the caregiver's eyes, I whispered, "Thank you, Doc, for helping me." I then glanced upwards toward the ceiling and silently prayed, "Lord, thank you once again for allowing me to escape the icy grip of death."

The doctor went on to describe my medical condition. He indicated that it was simply a miracle that I'd somehow survived so much physical trauma. The medial team had been amazed by the results of my CAT scan. They had expected to find massive brain damage including hemorrhaging and swelling of my brain, yet the results proved negative. In addition to running a CAT scan, more than fifty X-rays of my entire body were reviewed as they tried to determine the severity of my bone fractures. Lastly, the caregivers had completed an MRI on my massive shoulder injury.

The doctor continued his summary by telling me that I was presently in the surgical recovery room, following the first of my many subsequent surgical procedures. The surgery had involved putting my dislocated left shoulder and arm back into the proper alignment. I swallowed hard as he graphically continued to describe the internal havoc that I had invoked upon my body from the previous night of terror.

The list of my bone fractures was extensive. I had three broken vertebrae in my back. The right side of my rib cage was nearly collapsed. On impact, I'd fractured every one of the frontal ribs plus I broke three of those same ribs in a different place on the backside of my rib cage. My right-side collarbone was shattered in five places, plus my right shoulder was partially dislocated and had suffered severely torn cartilage. I also had fractured of my left leg. Furthermore, I broke the finger joints of my left thumb and forefinger. Lastly, I broke and lost some the main molars from my jaw.

The doctor said that further X-rays would probably discover more fractures and injuries. He was especially concerned about three of my scores of many injuries. The doctor shared that I would need several future surgeries. He went on to describe how badly the motorcycle accident had destroyed my left shoulder. During the impact, my left arm and shoulder socket had been dislodged. An extensive surgery would be required to not only rebuild my shoulder joint, but I'd severed all four of my rotator-cuff tendons and dislocated my bicep tendon, leaving my entire left arm virtually paralyzed. The doctor further explained that my multiply fractured collarbone would likely require surgical plates and pins to mend it. Lastly, he described his frightening prognosis of the multiple fractures in my back. The doctor was quite positive that I would require back surgery to fuse my damaged vertebrae and spine back together.

As the doctor paused, I contemplated my future. I thought to myself that perhaps it would have been better to die out in the desert rather than suffer from so many life-altering injuries.

The doctor spoke once again saying, "I know that your pain must be unbearable, but you should be happy to have survived. It is important though that you prepare yourself for the consequences of your accident. I'm going to predict that you will eventually recover, but you need to prepare yourself to accept that your life will never be the same again. Following your many surgeries, you'll likely have limited spinal mobility, limited arm mobility, and you'll likely walk with a limp for the rest of your future. I know this may be hard for you to handle right now, but you'll likely suffer from chronic pain and may require pain medications for the rest of your life."

The doctor left my side after mentioning that he would check back on me after I'd been relocated to my own hospital room. I silently thought to myself, I've heard pessimistic predictions from doctors in the past. Although I likened my doctor's description as proclaiming that my glass was half-empty, I made up my mind that my glass was instead half-full. Even so, one had to wonder if what I had done to myself would be worth the price I would have to pay.

Once the doctor had left my sight, I instantaneously began weighing my options. There were two distinct choices. I could succumb to the belief of only negative outcomes waiting in my future, and then fall into a deeply depressed state of self-pity, or I could fight for everything within my power to recover. I chose the latter since I've always believed that my one of my greatest strengths lies in my positive attitude and intensity to attain the goals, I've established for myself.

It was settled then; I promised myself that I would overcome my difficulties and would eventually take delight in proving the fact that my medical prognosis was far too gloomy for someone such as me.

By the time that I was relocated to my own hospital room, my mind was fixed on how to beat the odds of such a crippling motorcycle accident that nearly cost me my life. Before long, the doctor was once more stationed alongside my hospital bed. The time had arrived for me to influence my own medical outcome.

As the doctor reviewed my medical charts, I began our dialogue by asking, "Doc, how long would you speculate that I'll have to remain in your hospital?"

The doctor looked up from the chart and responded, "Well, I'm going to predict that you will be here for at least three or four weeks and perhaps up to six weeks. Your shoulder joint surgery that we just completed will be all that we can schedule for you this week. Next week, we will schedule the surgical procedure on your broken back, and then in the remaining few weeks, I predict we will complete your collarbone and leg surgeries."

With stone-cold seriousness, I said, "Doc, I don't mean you any disrespect, and I sincerely appreciate the lifesaving tactics that you and your staff provided me. I'm telling you that there is simply no way that I'm going to spend the next month or more lying in a Nevada hospital bed, which is one thousand five hundred miles away from my home back in Minnesota. I'll be honest with you, when I say that I'm very concerned about breaking my back in three locations, I'm not as concerned about any of my other extensive bone fractures, but I am perplexed about my back injuries."

The doctor stared at me with wonder and shared, "You should be extremely concerned about all of your injuries, but yes, particularly your spinal fractures."

I replied, "What I want to know, Doc, is what if I were to have my youngest son Travis drive throughout the day and night in order to arrive at this hospital room by tomorrow morning, will I risk paralysis if I get out of this bed and then travel back to Minnesota in my son's car?"

The doctor's face turned a shade of crimson. He was incensed as he retorted, "You must still be delirious. You don't seem to grasp the severity of your injuries. I can assure you that there will be no way that you will be physically able to get out of your hospital bed for at least a couple weeks. Even if you could, the only way to transport you back to a Minnesota hospital care unit would be by using a long-distance ambulatory carrier capable of meeting your medical needs during such an extensive 1,500-mile trip."

I redirected my question again and asked, "You didn't answer my question about paralysis if I get out of this bed tomorrow."

The doctor was unable to mask his frustration with my perseverance.

He sternly commented, "Alright, theoretically, if you could somehow miraculously get out of this bed tomorrow, it's not probable that you will paralyze yourself. As a result of your accident, you crushed three vertebrae in your spine so you'll endure pain like you've never experienced, but since you fortunately did not sever your spinal cord, you will not likely suffer paralysis. What you can't seem to comprehend is that you viciously impacted your body with a blunt-force trauma like smashing yourself into a solid brick wall while traveling at a blistering speed of seventy-five miles per hour. You can dream all you desire, but I can assure you that by tomorrow morning when you think you want to leave our intensive care unit, the front of your entire body will be bruised nearly the color of black all the way from your head down to your toes. You might think you'll have the fortitude to get up and leave our medical facility, but it simply isn't going to be possible."

I responded with, "Doc, I'm not going to argue with you because if you can't make me stay, then I want you to give me a signed medical release so I can go home tomorrow."

The doctor stormed out of my room snapping back with, "Oh, I'll give you your medical release alright, but you'll discover tomorrow the reason why you won't be going anywhere. It will be unfortunate that your son will have to drive all this way only to find out that you are bedridden!"

At the doctor left, my nurse sheepishly entered the room. I could tell that she wasn't used to a patient causing such a stir. Since both of my damaged arms were immobilized by arm slings and then strapped tightly to my chest, I asked the nurse for her help in making a phone call to my wife. The thoughtful nurse entered the phone number and then held the phone to my ear. After only one ring on the other end, my wife picked up the phone in a panic. I could hear her mixed sobs of happiness and relief as I shared all the details. At the conclusion of our conversation, my loving wife prepared to implement the logistics for an escape from my Nevada hospital incarceration the very next morning.

My son, Travis, and his wife, RaeLynn, unselfishly drove throughout the entire night allowing them to arrive at the Nevada hospital by 10:00 a.m. the day after my accident. The time was almost exactly twenty-four hours from when my doctor had stomped out of my room in anger. On my bedside stand lay the signed medical release from the disgruntled doctor, and the hospital's legal department granting me permission to depart from their care facility, along with my signed statement agreeing to release the hospital and its staff from any further responsibility or liability due my personal decision for a premature departure from emergency medical care.

The joy I felt watching my son and his wife enter my hospital room was indescribable. Though severely injured, my spirits elevated the instant they arrived. I was somewhat taken back, however, because following closely behind Travis and RaeLynn were my entire medical team consisting of two doctors and four nurses. As all six of them lined up along the far wall of my room, it suddenly dawned on me that my caregiver audience was there to witness my failed attempt at leaving their hospital.

I caught Travis's eye and then motioned for him to step alongside the opposite side of my bed. He did as I instructed and then I motioned that he places his ear next to my mouth.

With my son's ear close to my lips, I gently whispered, "Travis, I'm hurt bad, but I need to get out of this hospital and go back home to Minnesota with you and RaeLynn. As you can see, the doctors and nurses don't believe I can do this, but I'm going to prove them wrong. This won't be easy since I have a broken back, broken ribs, a broken collarbone, a broken leg, and both my arms are immobilized, so I'll need you to help sit me up in this bed, Travis."

Travis straightened up and gave me a questioning look, and then he bent over placing his lips alongside my ear and whispered, "Dad, you are broken everywhere on your body. Where exactly am I supposed to grab you to help you up and out of this bed without damaging you further?"

Once more, I motioned Travis to bring his ear toward my mouth as I whispered, "I want you to use your hand to grab the backside of my head. I'm going to count to three, and then I'm going to grit my teeth as you thrust me up into a sitting position. Whatever you do though, please don't let go of my head. I'm guessing the intense pain will probably cause me to pass out for a moment."

Such an absurd request to anyone other than a member of my family would have been considered sheer lunacy, but for Travis, it seemed a perfectly normal intention coming from me.

Travis readied himself, and at the count of three, I braced for the onslaught of pain. Just as I was propelled into the sitting position, the stabbing pain in my back became so intense that the room began spinning, and I was blinded by a bright white light as I lost consciousness momentarily. As promised, Travis held tightly onto the back of my head as my body went limp. It took a few unsettled moments, but my vision cleared, and the pain dulled slightly. Travis gingerly helped me to the edge of the bed just as an absurd thought crossed my mind.

With all the force I could muster, I shouted in the direction of the medical staff saying, "I've got two dozen broken bones including and a broken leg. Would someone please be kind enough to get me a wheelchair, or would you prefer that my son drags me out of this hospital?"

I'd scored one small victory, but my long battle to recover was only beginning.

Travis and RaeLynn helped me into the summoned wheelchair and then gently pushed me out of the hospital emergency room entrance. With great difficulty, my loved ones helped me out of the wheelchair and then lowered me down into the front seat of their compact Volkswagen car. Nothing like being critically injured, and then riding in style!

We were about to embark on a fifteen-hundred-mile journey that would require me to endure twenty-eight straight hours of nearly unbearable discomfort and pain, but at least I'd be home with my loved ones. Travis had no sooner maneuvered his little car away from the hospital when I shared some unsettling information with him. Just prior to leaving the hospital, one of my nurses had discussed some sensitive medical advice with me so I passed it on to my son.

I said, "Travis, one of my nurses mentioned that I would have to be very careful with my digestive system. She said it was concerning that I'd gone nearly forty-eight hours without food or drink, and then went through various surgical processes. She indicated to me that if I didn't find a way to avoid becoming constipated, I would suffer a great deal. Evidently because I've broken so many bones in my upper torso, she felt that I'd be in too great a pain struggling with a difficult bowel movement."

Travis looked at me and said, "Wow, that was more information than I really needed right now."

I said, "I'm sorry, but she mentioned that I needed to instruct you to stop somewhere along our travels to buy me some industrial-strength laxatives so I can avoid any problems. You don't have to stop and buy me some laxatives though until we need to stop for fuel somewhere down the road."

Suddenly, another daunting thought crossed my mind as I turned toward Travis and said, "Oh no, I just thought of something. With my extensive arm injuries, I can't even move my arms or hands. I'm not too high on this idea, but I'm afraid that whenever I do need to use the toilet, you are going to have to wipe my rear end, Travis!"

I'll never forget what happened next. We were cascading down the highway at the posted speed of seventy-five miles per hour when suddenly my son jerked the steering wheel of his car hard to right to take the final off-ramp exit before departing the city. I distinctly remember that instant as I cried out in pain by the car's erratic motion jarring my damaged body. In an apparent panic, Travis rapidly maneuvered the car into the parking lot of a large retail outlet store. With a stern look on his face and without speaking a word, he slammed on the brakes, bringing the car to a stop near the entrance.

As my son bolted from the car, I shouted, "Travis, I told you that it wasn't necessary to buy my laxatives until the next fuel stop."

I looked toward RaeLynn and said, "Why is he acting so irrational?"

After only a short wait, Travis returned carrying a large box that he hoisted into the back end of his car. Without saying a word and with a deep frown on his forehead, he took control of his car and once again guided the car back onto the highway.

Finally, I said, "What on earth are you so upset about, and what is in the large box that you just purchased in that store? That doesn't look like a box of laxatives to me."

While sternly hunching over his steering wheel, my son replied, "I got your dumb laxatives, but I also bought a large case of rubber gloves because there is no way I'm going to wipe your butt with my bare hands!"

With all my substantial injuries and even though my broken ribs made the act of moving, breathing, coughing, sneezing, or laughing an unbearable experience, I still broke out in laughter.

With both tears of joy and tears of pain running down my cheeks, I said to Travis, "You've got to be kidding me. When you were a baby, I changed your diapers and wiped your backside over and over again. I would think that my son would at least be willing to return the favor to help his old man out in my time of need."

The frown never left Travis's brow as he commented, "Say anything that you want, but I'm still not going to touch your butt with my hands."

****

It took twenty-eight hours of nonstop driving to bring me one thousand five hundred miles back to my home. By having my son transport me in his fuel-efficient "mini car," the total cost was around two hundred dollars for fuel and food. Had I been transported by ambulance the same distance, the tally would have surpassed fifty thousand dollars!

Shortly after arriving back at my home, we received the first of countless medical bills, which invariably left my wife and me in a state of "sticker shock." The first invoice we received was to pay for my emergency helicopter rescue. The costs allocated an astounding one-thousand-dollar-per-minute fee for each minute I was airborne inside the helicopter. From the moment that I was loaded onto the helicopter until it flew twenty-five miles to the emergency hospital and until I was removed totaled a mere sixteen minutes. The resulting invoice identified that we were to pay sixteen thousand dollars!

For the next several months following my accident, I went through an array of seven surgical procedures. In all, I required one CAT scan, three MRI scans, and more than one hundred and fifty X-rays. Following each surgery, I endured a daily regimen of new and evermore painful physical therapy that would have made even the toughest individual cringe in pain. The total medical expense for my care tallied more than one hundred and fifty thousand dollars. With each breath I continued to take, I'm in awe of the wonders of modern medicine's abilities to heal the wounded or save the dying, but medical miracles do not come without cost.

For months, I worked with several different teams of medical specialists. Those surgeons performed surgeries on each of my two shoulders, on my back, and on my leg. Each of four different doctors predicted that I would recover from my extensive injuries and continue to live a life with some semblance of normalcy. Each doctor, however, predicted that I would never ride a motorcycle ever again. The doctors based those predictions on sound medical knowledge since both of my shoulder joints were extremely damaged and the multiple fractures of my back would make future motorcycling impossible.

One day following the second of my three overall shoulder surgeries, I asked my doctor what it would take for me to ride a motorcycle again. He was taken aback by my request since most motorcycle crash victims are simply joyous to be alive and seldom ever attempt riding again.

I said, "Doc, riding a motorcycle is one of my most cherished life activities, and you've got to tell me what it will take to ride again."

My doctor replied, "Scott, your left shoulder joint has been so badly destroyed that I'm going to predict you'll only ever regain forty percent of your arm motion. You simply won't be able to raise your arms high enough to grasp the handlebars of a motorcycle. Regarding your broken back, you are destined for a lifetime of chronic back pain from your injuries, so riding a motorcycle is simply out of the question."

I retorted, "Doc, I'm going to ride again, so what will it require of me?"

The doctor spelled out a physical therapy regime that appeared impossible. He instructed me to meet with a professional therapist named Dan Ness who would help me understand my daunting task to fully recover.

The first time I met Dan, my assigned physical therapist, I was taken aback by his sheer size. Dan was a big man who had played college football years earlier.

His first words to me as he read my medical charts were, "Interesting. Your charts indicate that you have a high pain tolerance. Is that true?"

I responded, "Well, throughout all my recent injuries and following all past and present surgeries, I've never taken any form of pain medication. I can also tell you that I've never used Novocain whenever a dentist has drilled my teeth, so yes, I do have a high pain tolerance."

Dan narrowed his eyes and smugly commented, "I've had tough guys like you give similar responses, but they are usually the first ones to cry like a baby when I start breaking down their scar tissue or forcing their frozen joints back into motion. Hop up on this table, and let's see just how much pain tolerance you can endure he said with an evil smirk on his face."

As I lay down on the table, I retorted, "Knock yourself out because you are never going to get me to cry out, and I'm never going to beg you to stop inflicting your sadistic pain on me. I know what it will take to fully recover, and I intend on staying the course."

As Dan and I worked together over the course of many months, he and I became good friends with a high level of respect for each other. With each passing week, my recovery rate was far more than most patients. Both Dan and my doctors were spellbound by my commitment and work ethic to recover. They were amazed that I was willing to rise each day at 4:00 a.m. and then put myself through two hours of painful physical therapy. I endured this every day for nine long months. During each session, I would twist and pull and lift and stretch every injured portion of my body. I had to do back physical therapy, I had to do left and right shoulder physical therapy, I had to do left leg physical therapy, and I had to do strength and mobility exercises until the sweat poured from my body and until the self-inflicted pain became almost unbearable to endure.

As I met with Dan and my doctors for one final time nine long months after my life-threatening accident, they said, "Scott, you have been one of the most amazing patients that we've ever encountered. Seldom have we had a patient with so much drive and determination to overcome their injuries. You have nearly fully recovered, and you somehow found a way to beat all the odds."

I sincerely thanked them for all their contributions toward my recovery. I shook Dan's hand and then with a devious smile I said, "You never could get me to cry out or beg you to stop, could you? I'm sure, though, that would have given you immense joy."

Before departing from my doctor's examination room, I asked, "Doc, am I now cleared to ride a motorcycle again since springtime has arrived and a new riding season is upon us?"

My doctor said, "I thought it impossible when we first started your medical care, but unbelievably, you have regained nearly all your joint mobility and rebuilt all your atrophied muscles. If you must, start riding that a motorcycle again, but try to stay in one piece, will you?"

****

On that very next spring following the year of my accident, I bought another Harley-Davidson motorcycle to replace the one that had been destroyed in the accident. During that riding season, I logged more than twenty-five thousand miles upon my new motorbike and then I took great pride by informing all my "naysayer" doctors and friends. I'd done the impossible and was free to enjoy my life once more. At present, I'm fully recovered with no lasting effects of from my near-death experience. Miraculously, I have no back pain, nor do I suffer from any other painful aftermath because of my injuries. Whenever anyone becomes aware of my story of victory, they are amazed that I lack any outward signs of injury or that I'm not wrought by chronic pain. The only physical indicators of my brush with death are the countless surgical scars that are riddled across my body. What a small price to pay for the wonders of modern medicine.

****

It may seem that my story had reached a conclusion. It appeared that I'd mostly benefited from nothing more than a man-made victory over death. But I've saved how the Lord's influence helped me conquer death until the very last of this account. Here is the rest of the chronicle as it played out.

A few weeks following my critical accident, I received an accident report in the mail from the Nevada State Highway Patrol. The report included photos of the accident scene and outlined in graphic detail just how close I'd come to the brink of death. The documentation showed each deep divot in the sand made by my motorcycle as it flipped end for end for distance of one hundred and sixty feet. The report detailed how during the initial frontward flip; the headlight of my motorcycle was subsequently discovered driven deep into the sand after being sheared off. During the tumultuous ride as I held on for my very life, the back end of the motorcycle forcefully smashed into my spine time and again. With each revolution, the lethal machine left a telltale mark across my back while fracturing my vertebrae in three locations. Nearly every detail of the accident was vividly described, yet nowhere could I locate the mention of the mystery man who initially discovered me, and in the end, I believed he had helped save my life.

As soon as I studied the official accident report, without haste, I made a phone call to the Nevada State Highway Patrol office. I asked for the name and a phone number of the man who'd found me so that I might contact him and properly thank him. I was informed that there was no record of anyone finding me.

I stated, "For a moment when I'd regained consciousness while laying out in that desert, a stranger came to my aide. Are you saying that no one was at the scene of the accident when emergency help arrived?"

The officer on the other end of the phone said, "No. There was no one other than the medical crew and patrol officers present at the scene of your accident. I would suggest that you contact the Nevada 911 emergency network to determine who called in your accident."

Without haste, I called the Nevada 911 and inquired, "My name is Scott Gottschalk, and on June 30, 2009, I had a near-fatal motorcycle accident while traveling through Nevada. Sometime around 6:30 a.m. on that day I was aroused from a state of unconsciousness by a mystical stranger. My vision was unclear, so I can't identify much about the stranger, but I know someone came to my aide. I'm calling you so I can find out the name and phone number of that stranger, and then I can properly thank him for helping to save my life. Unfortunately, my official accident report doesn't include any information about the stranger, so it was suggested that I call you for more information."

The response shocked me when the 911 operator said, "We can't provide you with that information because on that morning our 911 dispatch received an abrupt call lasting only a few seconds."

The 911 operator went on to say that the only recorded 911 messages on record say, "Critical motorcycle accident at I-80 mile marker 324. Send help." With that, the phone disconnected without being able to track the caller's phone number or identification.

The operator's tone firmed while saying, "A caller disconnecting from a 911 call is improper protocol. No one is supposed to hang up on a 911 emergency call until we release them, for the very reason that we want to identify the caller, get specifics of the emergency, and so on. All we can tell you is that yes someone left a brief message, but we have no documentation of who it was or how you could go about contacting them. In fact, we'd surmised it was likely a prank call."

As I hung up the phone, I struggled with what I'd heard. How was it possible that a mystery stranger was there only to disappear without record? After all of that, one would think the stranger would have at least invested enough time to ensure my rescue. I've continually been at odds with this anomalous outcome. Why did the stranger appear then disappear without a clue? I couldn't be seen by any passing cars from where I'd been thrown out into the desert, yet in my foggy mindset, I felt a presence of a very out-of-focus individual. Still no footprints were discovered in the sand near my accident wreckage. Who or what was it?

I have a theory that has forevermore instilled in me a belief in guardian angels. Hardly a day goes by since my tragic accident that I don't think about the moment the stranger startled me back from the brink of death. With each passing day, I more firmly believe that the stranger may not have been a real person at all.

Was the mystical stranger even a person at all, or was it an angel sent from God who startled me back into life?

With each passing year of my life, my faith continues to build. I've had far too many unexplainable circumstances to discount divine intervention. On that fateful day, I should never have survived, yet I did. I should never have fully recovered from my extensive injuries, but I have. I want to tell all who read these words, that I've witnessed angels, and I've felt the loving hand of the Lord nudging me onward in life.

This is my witness and testimony. I believe in angels.

CHAPTER 6

Pushing Limits

I've described some of my personal triumph over certain death. The will to survive had motivated my behavior to conquer permanent disablement and then continue living my life with intensity as never before. Through an astonishing dedication and commitment, and by never losing faith, I attained a full recovery enabling me to beat all the odds. During my recuperation, I demonstrated to all the doubters that almost any physical limitation can be overcome through the power of positive thinking, a dedicated work ethic, and a belief in the power of prayer. Inexplicable miracles surface all the time.

****

As the new motorcycle-riding season arrived exactly one year removed from the date of my near demise, I had made all the physical, the mental, and the mechanical preparations to ride a motorcycle once more. There was little doubt that I'd been given yet another chance to participate in the many experiences and pleasures that life can offer.

Prior to beginning a renewed motorcycle-riding season, I contemplated the numerous guardian angels that had mystically aided me during my times of trouble. In a somewhat humorous tribute to those angels, which I sincerely believe were sent to me by God, I bought, and then permanently installed a tiny symbolic "guardian angel" bell underneath the frame of my motorcycle. Once in place, this bell continuously tolls while the motorcycle is in operation.

Motorcycle legend has it that a small bell attached to one's motorcycle, positioned close to the ground, catches the "evil road spirits." The little demons living on one's motorcycle cause all kinds of mechanical problems and life-threatening mayhem. The cavity of the bell attracts these evil spirits, but the constant ringing drives them insane, whereby they lose their grip and then fall to the ground. In turn, their fall onto the roadway is a major cause of potholes developing in the road.

Okay, perhaps the legend is a bit far-fetched, but from my perspective, having one of those legendary "guardian angel" bells in place during any future motorcycle rides couldn't hurt.

****

My wife, Astrid, and I departed on our first motorcycle trip together since the events of my previous year's dreadful accident. The chosen route had a very special significance because we were traveling one thousand five hundred miles all the way back to the scene of my accident. I was drawn to return to the spot that nearly killed me so that I could put some closure on the matter.

After a few days' ride while covering fifteen hundred miles, we slowed as we reached the infamous mile marker 324 on Nevada Interstate Highway 80. I brought the motorcycle to a halt, and we walked with trepidation toward the sandy shoulder of the highway. We both looked toward the ground in disbelief as we discovered that the deep tracks from my motorcycle's accident were still embedded into the sand an entire year later. A chill went up my spine as we followed the trail leading out into the desert.

Along our trek, we detected the severed sagebrush that had initiated my motorcycle, and I to flip end for end for one hundred and sixty feet. It was spooky to be able to observe and sense the carnage that had occurred one year earlier.

I held Astrid's hand tightly within mine. Unable to contain her tears and her emotions, she cried, "Why weren't you taken from me? Looking at this rough terrain and seeing the path you took after hitting that deer with your motorcycle, I don't see how it would be possible for anyone to survive."

With my own outpour of emotions, I replied, "Only the Lord could have protected me that night, and I need to make my own private peace with him. Could you please walk back out to the highway and leave me alone for a moment?"

Once Astrid had turned and walked away, I dropped down to my knees in the exact spot where I nearly lost my life. I offered up a prayer of gratitude for my continued gift of life.

One year earlier, I had attempted to ride a motorcycle over three thousand miles by riding nonstop for forty-eight hours. The crash with a deer had stopped me in my tracks, nearly ending my life. Now, with a sense of renewal, Astrid and I departed for the Pacific Ocean to complete the long-distance endurance motorcycle ride that had escaped me one year earlier. I covered the remaining five hundred miles and with a passionate sense of fulfillment, and then I drew the sample of seawater that had eluded my previous year's endurance ride.

Due to factors beyond my control, I'd failed to complete my coastline-to-coastline ride across the USA at its widest point within the allotted forty-eight hours. Although it took me nearly one year and a near-death experience, I had finally completed my objective.

During our ensuing motorcycle vacation, my wife and I canvassed much of the beautiful western states. We safely covered over four thousand five hundred miles by the conclusion. As I fell into my zone of peaceful motorcycling miles, my confidence grew as I started "cooking up" my plans for another "extreme" long-distance motorcycle journey.

****

On that same summer from July 2 through July 11, I had a most unique and amazing opportunity to travel the highways and byways around our entire great nation. I choose to attempt what few motorcyclists have ever attempted.

As I've indicated previously, in my opinion, motorcycling has been and always will be the ultimate expression of personal freedom. As a biker, one is unrestricted albeit braving the elements with nothing but an unhindered view from all directions. There is no comparison versus how restricted the view is from inside an automobile as opposed to the glorious sights to behold from the seat of a motorbike cruising down the road with the wind, the sun, and the elements in your face. It has been said that motorcyclists are the only people on earth that fully appreciate why a dog sticks its head out the window of a vehicle while traveling at high speeds down the open road and then reflects an expression of pure joy upon its face.

As previously indicated, I'm a certified member of a long-distance motorcycle association, which consists of tens of thousands of long-distance endurance motorcycle riders from across the nation. This group endorses the belief that they are the toughest bikers on the planet for obvious reasons. Over the years, I've certified several endurance rides. Not only are the rides challenging, but the exorbitant documentation required to get one's ride qualified is a massive task.

These certified rides are not races but rather endorse lawful long-distance endurance motorcycle riding. While the distances traveled by motorcycle for some of the rides seem an impossible task, I assure you that certain riders such as me simply enjoy the challenge of seeking out and achieving their long-distance riding goals. Such rides stress safe, legal riding; however, the miles and the hours can be excessively long to be sure. Each certified long-distance ride typically requires two witnesses at the start and two witnesses at the end of a specific ride to document odometer readings, time, date, location, etc. Along the way, each credit card fuel receipt becomes a combined time card, odometer recording document, fuel consumption monitor, and speed monitoring benchmark for distances traveled between fuel stops.

To become a qualified member of the association, a motorcyclist must successfully complete an initial one-thousand-mile ride in under twenty-four hours. All IBA association members have certified at least this specific ride; however, only a fraction of the overall membership ever chooses to do another ride or anything remotely more difficult than one thousand miles within twenty-four hours. If a novice motorcycle long-distance rider endures such a ride, then they are at liberty to select other rides in which to certify. The next-level rides generally increase in difficulty and endurance. The first next-level ride is a one-thousand-five-hundred-mile ride, which must be completed in less than thirty-six hours.

If one desires to move on to even more challenging rides, one then enters another world of difficulty categorized as *EXTREME* rides. The first extreme ride requires that a biker must ride at least one thousand five hundred miles in less than twenty-four hours. If one does the math, it then means that a motorcyclist must average well over sixty miles per hour for twenty-four hours straight while still fitting in fuel stops, bathroom breaks, and taking in some nourishment and fluids. Once one enters the realm of extreme riding, extended sleep is not an option. This may seem dangerous, but some folks—me included—do very well on minimal sleep, however, the rules make it very clear that it is far better to stop and rest and simply not qualify your ride rather than to ride unsafe and tired, and then perhaps die trying to earn a cheap certificate to hang on the wall.

Next-level ever-more difficult rides requires starting in Canada, crossing through the border control, traveling over one thousand five hundred miles all the way through the widest portion of the USA and then crossing into Mexico in under twenty-four hours. This is a ride that many attempt but only a fraction are ever able to achieve because of the tight time restrictions required to achieve the goals of the ride and the ever-possible border crossing delays.

Perhaps the most challenging endurance ride of all time is the coastline-to-coastline ride. This is the specific ride in which I hit a deer in Nevada resulting in a horrific crash, which left me with dozens of fractured bones including breaking my back in three places. Overall, this demanded a lot of surgeries and physical therapy for me to become whole again. The specifics of this ride are that a motorcycle enthusiast begins on the East Coast by collecting a water sample of the Atlantic Ocean. The custom route that I chose involved an attempt to travel the widest portion of the USA and then cover over three thousand miles in less than forty-eight consecutive hours while averaging nearly seventy miles per hour to reach the West Coast. The end reward was to draw a final sample of water from the Pacific Ocean within the allotted time frame. Thus, ocean to ocean in under 48 hours.

To date, only a handful of riders have ever accomplished such a ride, and I'd hoped to join their elite status. For the record, on this ride before my near-fatal deer collision, I was on schedule to reach my goal under the time limit. I had covered more than two thousand five hundred miles in forty straight hours of driving, all while averaging nearly seventy miles per hour when the crash put a fast ending to my ultimate riding objective.

With the descriptions of the previous rides, I will share that I'm probably considered a true "hard-core" distance motorcycle rider. To date, I've completed more than forty various one-thousand-mile rides within a twenty-four-hour period. I've also completed nineteen separate one-thousand-five-hundred-mile rides within a twenty-four-hour period. In addition, I've successfully ridden a motorcycle from Canada to Mexico covering more than one thousand five hundred miles within a twenty-four-hour time frame. I've even unofficially completed a three-thousand-mile ride that would have been completed within a forty-eight-hour period, however, this specific attempt took me one year to come back and finish because of a deer collision with my motorcycle.

One of the most grueling of all the extreme rides is called the 10-10ths ride. This ride demands that the rider logs one thousand miles per twenty-four-hour day for ten consecutive days in a row. On July 2–11, 2010, I completed and certified that very, very difficult ride during one of the highest national holiday travel weeks for the entire year.

On day one, I obtained my two witnesses from a Harley-Davidson dealer at 1:00 p.m. on Friday, July 2, to begin the momentous task of attempting to drive more than ten thousand miles by motorcycle around the outside edge of the entire United States. I'd planned the route and trip for nearly three years. I had each evening's motel rooms reserved months prior to my departure. I even had appointments made weeks ahead with Harley-Davidson dealers in Texas, in Alabama, and in Florida to make quick stops during my route for any potential tire changes or service work.

The first challenge of the route occurred when I was forced against my will into an eight-hour delayed start because of a servicing lag performed by the Harley-Davidson dealership. They were unable to complete their service work on my bike in the promised time frame. Because it was impossible for me to rebook all ten nights of my motel rooms over the busy July Fourth Holiday week, I was only going to get back on schedule by skipping my first night of sleep and then driving nonstop to my second motel stay. So, in effect, day one rolled right into day two, which was like starting a massive endurance ride such as this with one foot in the grave so to speak. As result of these circumstances, both my wife and I were uneasy because of the previous year's catastrophic collision.

I traveled along my way on Interstate Highway 94 westbound through Minnesota, North Dakota, Montana, Idaho, Washington, and finally Oregon before stopping for the first time on my journey. For my combined first day one- and second-day legs of the ride, I logged more than twenty-one hundred continuous miles in under thirty-six hours. The most difficult part of the first leg of my trip other than the protracted hours without sleep was that in the Rocky Mountains of western Montana at about 2:00 a.m. I had to deal with 34-degree temperatures, along with hail, and an ice-cold rainfall.

Knowing that I had a lot of miles riding through a very populated area of California to travel the next day, I only slept about two hours, and then departed about 2:00 a.m. For day three, I rode through Oregon, California, Nevada, and ended up in Arizona for completion of my third consecutive one-thousand-mile day. I can't describe the beauty of nature that I witnessed while riding in solitude as each morning I saw dawn's early light peeking out from behind some beautiful mountain or rising out of the seemingly endless ocean waters. The most difficult part of this leg of the trip was that the temperatures climbed to over 110 degrees near Death Valley, and then I traveled over eight hundred miles through the deserts of Nevada where the temperature stayed at 105 degrees for most of the day.

On day four, I traveled through Arizona, New Mexico, and ended up at my motel stay in Texas. Along this route of the southwestern USA, I endured lots more high heat traveling, and due to the hurricane, which had recently made landfall near Texas, I was faced with countless hard-driving rains along this most southern USA route.

NO BOUNDARIES TOUR

On day five, I traveled through Texas, Louisiana, Mississippi, Alabama, and ended up in Florida for my motel stay. Once again, the driving rains as the hurricane aftermath made for some extremely difficult motorcycling.

On day six, I traveled all the way down to the bottom of Florida then back up the East Coast riding through Georgia, South Carolina, and ending up in North Carolina for a motel stay. On this day, I had a near tragic accident, which could have ended it all had my "guardian angel" once again not been by my side. As I traveled north on Interstate Highway 95, the highway went up and over a huge suspension bridge in Savannah, Georgia. The flow of traffic was speeding along at over seventy miles per hour and all around me were semitrucks traveling at full speed. As I neared the top of the massive bridge, a huge gust of wind blasted from my left side, which resulted in literally throwing my motorcycle to the right and into the semitruck while traveling at seventy miles per hour. I can't describe my feelings as my motorcycle impacted into the rear dual wheels of the thundering semitrailer. A mere motorcycle is no match for a semitruck, as the front faring of my cycle was smashed backwards into my engine and my foot floorboard was driven over by the truck wheels making it unusable. I impacted so hard with the truck that my sunglasses were knocked off my head. I used every ounce of adrenaline I could muster to keep my eight-hundred-pound motorcycle from falling beneath the semitruck wheels or, worse yet, crashing, only to be run over by the speeding traffic beside and behind me.

Somehow, I righted the disabled motorcycle even at such a high speed. I dare say that someone with much less riding experience most probably would have met their fate on that day, but I feel very blessed to have safely navigated such a close call. Once I could exit from the dangerous bridge, I stopped my motorcycle along the shoulder of the busy interstate highway to survey the damage and make some fixes to keep me traveling down the road once more.

By kicking and pounding with my legs, I was able to bend the twisted crash bar and my cracked faring far enough away from the engine to make the machine operable once again. As I think back, I wonder what the passing vehicles thought as they watched what appeared to be an extremely angry biker kicking the "you know what" out of his Harley motorcycle. I guess first impressions aren't always accurate.

Next, I used all my strength to somehow bend and twist my right-side floorboard up into a position so that I could at least continue to ride the machine, but it remained so uneven that riding the next several thousand miles was anything but comfortable. I was shocked to see how much truck tire rubber marks were imbedded into the right side of my motorcycle. In the end, my motorcycle had earned some more character as it reflected the scars from doing battle with a semitruck. My motorcycle was scratched, was twisted, and was broken in several places, but it kept going when the "chips were down." Upon returning home, I would discover that I had amassed over one thousand dollars in damage to my motorcycle, yet it kept driving for the thousands of miles it needed to complete the certified ride.

What are the odds that I had somehow skirted death one more time? How could anyone survive so many close calls and still be alive to talk about it? Some even began suggesting that I perhaps needed to start buying lottery tickets with all my luck!

On day seven, I traveled through North Carolina, Virginia, Maryland, New Jersey, Rode Island, Connecticut, Massachusetts, and ended up in New York for a motel stay. It was on this day that I nearly gave up on finishing my lofty goal of ten consecutive one-thousand-mile days. I cannot describe how difficult it was to travel more than one thousand miles per day then attempt it again and again, day after day, especially during one of the most nationwide traveled Independence Day holidays. It became evermore impossible with the population density, with the heavy flow

NO BOUNDARIES TOUR

of traffic, and with the never-ending road construction. Believe it or not, I hit Washington, DC, during the morning rush hour where I was forced to endure five hours of stop-and-go traffic trying to simply get beyond our nation's capital city. As luck would have it, I then hit afternoon rush hour traffic in New York City. At the time, the entire East Coast was encased by a heatwave during this time, so at 4:00 p.m. in 103-degree temperatures, I was gridlocked in traffic for over six hours. The heat coming off my air-cooled Harley engine while sitting endlessly in traffic nearly left me ill from heat exposure. At one point, to try to stop my air-cooled Harley engine from cooking itself, I was forced to shut down the motorcycle engine, and even in the searing heat, I was forced to push the motorcycle nearly one mile simply using my legs since the traffic was moving only a few feet at any given time.

I had reached my lowest point during the entire journey. It began to dawn on me that my ten-thousand-mile motorcycle riding target was perhaps unattainable. I suddenly looked in my rearview mirror and noticed a so-called "Crotch Rocket" motor biker come weaving in and out of traffic almost sounding and looking like a big mosquito as he navigated his way up through the endless view of seemingly stalled cars. At that point, I planned to follow suit. I wasn't sure if what the other biker was doing was exactly legal, but I could no longer risk inflicting permanent engine and transmission damage to my Harley.

A smile crossed my face as a comical thought came to me. If the car drivers compared his motions to be that of a nimble mosquito darting in and out, then perhaps they envisioned me and my big Harley to appear as a big, huge hippopotamus! While I was able to navigate the path of the darting "Crotch Rocket," I couldn't go nearly as fast as his nimble motorcycle could. I was shocked as he began watching out for me, as he made sure that I could keep up with his lead. We had become biker teammates doing battle together.

Mile after mile, we worked our way up through the densely stalled mass of vehicles seemingly stalled upon the New York City highways. Suddenly my new biker friend quickly pulled his motorcycle back into a nearly stalled driving lane where I slid in next to him. It was then for the first time that we exchanged conversations, and he mentioned that he was quite impressed that a Harley rider would have anything to do with a "Crotch Rocket" rider. I smiled back at him and asked why we had pulled back into the lane of cars rather than darting in and out on the shoulders of the highway just as we'd been doing for miles. He stated that just around the corner up ahead would be a patrol car waiting to give someone a driving violation. Sure enough, we crawled slowly past a lurking squad car, only to scamper once again upon our journey when the law officer was out of our vision once again. At the time that young biker was my new best friend in the entire world as he assisted me to navigate through a nearly impossible scenario in a traffic-grid-locked New York City.

Somehow, I endured the most physically demanding day of riding a motorcycle that I've ever encountered. That one-thousand-mile day began for me at 3:00 a.m. and ended a staggering twenty-three hours later at 2:00 a.m. I simply cannot describe how difficult doing something like that was with the temperatures more than 100 degrees and then trying to remain safe on one of the most congested series of highways in all of America. Not once during any of those searing high temperatures did my "nonexistent" air-conditioning system work!

In conditions such as those, it was impossible to take in enough fluids to remain hydrated, and I had little time to consume any real nutrients on any given day. For the most part, I survived my ten-day ride by eating protein and power bars throughout each day. The problem arose, however, when my electrolyte balance must have become very unstable by about day four of my endurance test. From that day forward, I suffered severe muscle-cramping in the calves, thighs, and hamstring muscles of my legs every night. The overall pain was excruciating to say the least.

On day eight, I traveled through New York, Pennsylvania, Ohio, Indiana, Illinois, and stayed at a motel in Iowa. The number of tolls I had to pay to use the roads in the eastern half of the USA was staggering. The tolls just for my motorcycle on this trip tallied over seventy-five dollars. As if dealing with two severe rush-hour traffic jams on the prior day in both Washington, DC, and in New York City, within the same 36-hour period wasn't bad enough; I also then ran into the afternoon rush hour of Chicago nonetheless. Once again, I was mired down in a sweltering heat wave as the traffic barely inched forward. For the record, I implemented some of my "Crotch Rocket" friend's maneuvers to reduce the agony somewhat. Later that night at about 1:30 a.m., I called my wife to let her know that I'd safely made it through another difficult and challenging day.

As I shared, I mockingly said to her, "I'm lying on my motel bed in the fetal position while sucking my thumb because of the stress. I've had to endure the three worst rush-hour cities in the nation, and I encountered then all within a thirty-six-hour time frame."

We both got a little chuckle because of my plight.

On day nine, I traveled onward through Iowa, Nebraska, and Wyoming before stopping to spend my final night with my son, Travis, his wife, RaeLynn, and my new granddaughter, Hiltina. On this ninth day of seemingly endless one-thousand-mile days, all I could think about was praying and hoping it would all be over soon. I had hit the wall so to speak with my energy tank nearing complete empty. By that point of my trip, it was difficult to determine what was keeping me going. I was physically depleted and mentally spent since the average day of operating my motorcycle was always somewhere between nineteen to twenty-three continuous hours. Each night, I would stagger into a hotel room between midnight to 2:00 a.m. At the end of each day, I would take a quick shower to remove an elongated day's worth of road grime from my body. I would then sleep a mere two hours before heading back out onto the road again by 2:00 a.m. to 3:00 a.m.

On the tenth and final day, I departed once again at 2:00 a.m. traveling through Wyoming, Montana, back through Wyoming, South Dakota, and finally I arrived back at my home in the state of Minnesota. On that day, my spirits were uplifted knowing that with every mile I was drawing ever closer to my ending objective. Travel became easier as well because of the reduced volume of traffic within the mid sections of our country. Such had not been the case while riding throughout the populated outside edges the previous nine days.

OVERALL SUMMARY OF 10-DAY TRIP:

- Daily certified motorcycling mileage tally was:

    - Day one: 1,053 miles
    - Day two: 1,043 miles
    - Day three: 1,049 miles
    - Day four: 1,025 miles
    - Day five: 1,049 miles
    - Day six: 1,011 miles
    - Day eight: 1,019 miles
    - Day nine: 1,076 miles
    - Day ten: 1,038 miles

- Grand total: 10,382 miles
- Total states ridden: 34
- It took 76 gas fills using 307 gallons of fuel for a cost of $917.
- Average fuel efficiency was 33.8 mpg.
- Logged +20 hours per day average (+200 hours in ten days)

- My Harley ran nearly nonstop for ten days and nights for over 10,000 miles without any mechanical difficulties. The engine required only two-thirds of a quart of oil for the entire trip. As a result of my extensive trip, I became more confident than ever that a Harley motorcycle can handle as many high-distance miles as any brand of motorcycle in the market.
- Averaged 2 hours per night sleep.
- Total motel stops cost $346.
- Total food and beverage cost $200.
- Total toll fees cost $76.
- Grand total trip cost: $1,538.
- Overall experience and self-satisfaction: PRICELESS!!

By successfully completing a long-distance endurance motorcycling trip of such magnitude allowed me to fulfill one of my lifelong dreams. Few people could understand why anyone would even attempt something so challenging and painful. In my lifetime, I've struggled through some immense challenges, but completing more than ten thousand miles within a ten-day time frame ranked as one of the three most difficult experiences that I've ever put myself through.

Again, I would liken such an extreme motorcycle ride to be like someone's attempt to climb Mount Everest or someone's attempt to run a marathon. Each of us has a right to set our own goals. Why should anyone else judge another's goals as being unwise, unsafe, or unattainable? I believe that personal goals are important, and the negative-induced thoughts of others shouldn't count for much in the overall scheme of things.

In all honesty, the tortuous act of completing such an extensive endurance ride was anything but fun. Still, I'll never forget the moments of pure exhilaration as I experienced the entire United States within a mere ten days. In my past, I've been fortunate enough to travel several times throughout all fifty states and I've experienced nearly all the tourist-trap activities. During each of those previous trips, I covered only a small portion of our great and wonderful nation. For this unique journey, however, I was able to breath in the glorious magnitude, the grandeur, and the sheer beauty that our land beholds, all while canvassing its entirety within only ten days. The experience provided a perspective of our nation that I'd never captured before.

    In the end, I'm only concerned with how I measure up to my own personal standards of living life to the fullest. I'm more than content to accept that I'm merely a common human who dreams big and thinks outside the box of normalcy. Through grit and self-determination, I've been able to accomplish some very uncommon feats that few on this planet could match. I guess if it were easy, then everyone would be capable of doing it.

CHAPTER 7

Years Planning World Record

WORLD RECORD BIKE RIDE CHARITY FUNDRAISER
RIDE DETAILS PASSED ALONG TO POTENTIAL SPONSORS

No Boundaries Tour
"Stop Human Trafficking"

Pledge any single dollar amount/person = $_____ Donation/person
Pledge $10/10,000 miles = $120 Donation/person
Pledge $.005 (1/2 cent)/mile X 120,000 miles = $600 Donation/person
Pledge $.01 (1 cent)/mile X 120,000 miles = $1,200 Donation/person

Guinness Record-Setting Motorcycle Ride

120,000 miles in under 120 days of continuous +1,000 miles/day all within one country

Other IBA Qualifying Rides could be gained along the way:

- IBA Record-Breaking Ride (Saddle-Sore SS120,000 miles in <120 days in one year, 1 man, 1 motorcycle)
- 100K Club (100,000 miles in one year)
- 45/45 Challenge (45 days - 45,000 miles)

- 40/40 Challenge (40 days - 40,000 miles)
- Longest Month (30/31 days - 30,000 miles)
- 20/20 Insanity (20 days - 20,000 miles)
- 10/10ths (10 days - 10,000 miles)
- Saddle-Sore 1,000 (24 hours - 1,000 miles) X 120 days = 120,000 miles

Proposed thirteen state route with a continuous 5-day 5,180-mile rotational loop:

- 1st Day of rotation:
    - **Night in St. Cloud, MN** > Butte, MT (18 hours) - **1,016 miles**
- 2nd Day of rotation:
    - **Night in Butte, MT** > Sioux Falls, SD > Watertown, SD > Watertown, SD (18 hours) - **1,035 miles**
- 3rd Day of rotation:
    - **Night in Watertown, SD** > Fargo, ND > Butte, MT > Belgrade, MT (18 hours) - **1,047 miles**
- 4th Day of rotation:
    - **Night in Belgrade, MT** > Buffalo, WY > Cheyenne, WY > Lincoln, NE (18 hours) - **1,056 miles**
- 5th Day of rotation:
    - **Night in Lincoln, NE** > Omaha, NE > Sioux City, IA > Pembina, ND > - **1,028 miles**
    - Casselton, ND > St. Cloud, MN (18 hours)

TOTAL MILES IN 5-Day ROTATIONAL LOOP (1,035-mile average per day): 5,180 miles

- May 25–31, 2025 - 7 days
- June 1–30, 2025 - 30 days
- July 1–31, 2025 - 31 days
- August 1–31, 2025 - 31 days
- September 1–18, 2025 (70th Birthday Celebration) - 18 days

NO BOUNDARIES TOUR

TOTAL Proposed Continuous Riding Days to Complete: 117-120 days

- 23 trips (5 days) X 5,180 miles = 119,140 miles
- + (1 day) Miami > Louisville (1,083 mi.) + (1 day) Louisville > St. Cloud (1,031 mi.) = 121,250 Total Miles

Ride Specifics
- 117–120 days X 1,030 mi/day X 65 mph ave = predicted 120,000 total miles (17-hour riding/7-hour downtime)
- 120,000 miles @ 35 mpg (5.5 gal. tank) = 3,500-gal (1,000 fills) X $6/gal. = **$21,000**
- 120,000 miles @ 35 mpg (10 gal. w/ fuel cell tank) = (400 fills)
- 12 full tire changes X $1,000 = **$12,000**
- 24 oil changes and service X $145 = **$ 3,500**
- 120 days food X $50 = **$ 6,000**
- Repairs and miscellaneous expenses = **$22,000**
- 94 nights motels X $110 = **$10,500**

TOTAL TRAVEL EXPENSES: $75,000
- 2023 (120th Anniversary HD Road Glide Limited) Motorcycle - **$50,000**

TOTAL TRIP INVESTMENT: $125,000

Routes
1. **Day One Route:**
   St. Cloud, MN to Butte, MT/1016 miles - **1,016**
2. **Day Two Route:**
   Butte, MT to Sioux Falls, SD/900 miles and Sioux Falls, SD to Watertown, SD/110 miles - **1,035**
3. **Day Three Route:**
   Watertown, SD to Fargo, ND/145 miles and Fargo, ND to Butte, MT/830 miles and Butte, MT to Belgrade, MT/85 miles - **1,047**

4. **Day Four Route:**
   Belgrade, MT to Buffalo, WY/310 miles and Buffalo, WY to Cheyenne, WY/300 miles and Cheyenne, WY to Lincoln, NE/445 miles - **1,056**
5. **Day Five Route:**
   Lincoln, NE to Omaha, NE/60 miles and Omaha to Sioux City, IA/95 miles and Sioux City, IA to Pembina, ND/475 miles and Pembina, ND to Casselton, ND/162 miles and Casselton, ND to St. Cloud, MN/213 miles - **1,028**
   Total Miles: 5,180

MapQuest Milage Routing

Auxiliary 1st Day:
- Miami, FL > Louisville, KY I-75N to I-64W to I-65N - **1,083 mi**

Auxiliary 2nd Day:
- Louisville, KY > St. Cloud, MN I-65N to I-74W to I-80W - **1,031 mi** to I-35N to I-94W

1st Day of Standard Rotation:
- St. Cloud, MN > Butte, MT I-94W to I-90W - **1,016 mi**

2nd Day of Standard Rotation:
- Butte, MT > Billings, MT I-94E - 225 mi
- Billings, MT > Sioux Falls, SD I-90E - 675 mi
- Sioux Falls, SD > Watertown, SD I-29N - 108 mi
   1,035 mi in total

3rd Day of Standard Rotation:
- Watertown, SD > Fargo, ND I-29N - 145 mi
- Fargo, ND>Butte, MT I-94W to I-90W - 830 mi
- Butte, MT>Belgrade, MT I-90E - 85 mi
   1,047 mi in total

NO BOUNDARIES TOUR

4th Day of Standard Rotation:
- Belgrade, MT > Buffalo, WY I-90E - 310 mi
- Buffalo, WY>Cheyenne, WY I-25S - 300 mi
- Cheyenne, WY>Lincoln, NE I-80E - 445 mi
  1,056 mi in total

5th Day of Standard Rotation:
- Lincoln, NE > Omaha, NE I-80E- 60 mi
- Omaha, NE > Sioux City, IA I-29N - 95 mi
- Sioux City, IA > Pembina, ND I-29N- 474 mi
- Pembina, ND > Casselton, ND I-29S to I-94W - 162 mi
- Casselton, ND > St. Cloud, MN I-94E to MN Hwy 15S - 213 mi
  1,028 mi in total

Standard (Every 5 Days) Rotation = 5,180 miles (120 days total = 4 mo.)
5,180 miles X 23 (Standard Rotations) = 119,140 miles (115 days total)
1,083 miles + 1,031 miles (2 Initial Auxiliary Days) = 2,114 miles (117–120 days predicted final)

*****Grand Total Continuous Biker Trip = 120,000 miles (<120 days)*****

SCOTT D. GOTTSCHALK

Guinness World Record Itinerary
2025 Dates and Stops

	DAY	MOTEL	MISC
0	Saturday, May 24	Miami, FL	**World Record Launch Gathering/Party**
1	Sunday, May 25	Louisville, KY	**3:00 a.m. begin Record Ride, 9:00 p.m. 1st Motel**
2	Monday, May 26	St. Cloud, MN	Holiday - **1st Bike Service (2,114 miles) oils**
3	Tuesday, May 27	Butte, MT	
4	Wednesday, May 28	Watertown, SD	
5	Thursday, May 29	Belgrade, MT	
6	Friday, May 30	Lincoln, NE	
7	Saturday, May 31	St. Cloud, MN	**2nd Bike Service (7,300 miles) oils**
8	Sunday, June 1	Butte, MT	
9	Monday, June 2	Watertown, SD	
10	Tuesday, June 3	Belgrade, MT	
11	Wednesday, June 4	Lincoln, NE	
12	Thursday, June 5	St. Cloud, MN	**3rd Bike Service (10,500 miles) oils**
13	Friday, June 6	Butte, MT	
14	Saturday, June 7	Watertown, SD	
15	Sunday, June 8	Belgrade, MT	
16	Monday, June 9	Lincoln, NE	
17	Tuesday, June 10	St. Cloud, MN	**4th Bike Service (13,700 miles) oils/tires**

18	Wednesday, June 11	Butte, MT	
19	**Thursday, June 12 (1,095)**	**Watertown, SD > Sisseton, SD**	
20	**Friday, June 13 (980)**	West Bend, WI	(Classic Green Reunion 2025: John Deere Conf.)
21	**Saturday, June 14 (1,070)**	West Bend, WI	(Keynote Speech at National JD Conference)
22	**Sunday, June 15 (995)**	**St. Cloud, MN**	**5th Bike Service (18,900 miles) oils**
23	Monday, June 16	Butte, MT	
24	Tuesday, June17	Watertown, SD	
25	Wednesday, June 18	Belgrade, MT	
26	Thursday, June 19	Lincoln, NE	
27	Friday, June 20	St. Cloud, MN	**6th Bike Service (24,100 miles) oils**
28	Saturday, June 21	Butte, MT	
29	Sunday, June 22	Watertown, SD	
30	Monday, June 23	Belgrade, MT	
31	Tuesday, June 24	Lincoln, NE	
32	Wednesday, June 25	St. Cloud, MN	**7th Bike Service (29,300 miles) oils/tires**
33	Thursday, June 26	Butte, MT	
34	Friday, June 27	Watertown, SD	

#	Day	Location	Service
35	Saturday, June 28	Belgrade, MT	
36	Sunday, June 29	Lincoln, NE	
37	Monday, June 30	St. Cloud, MN	**8th Bike Service (34,500 miles) oils**
38	Tuesday, July 1	Butte, MT	
39	Wednesday, July 2	Watertown, SD	
40	Thursday, July 3	Belgrade, MT	
41	Friday, July 4	Lincoln, NE	Holiday
42	Saturday, July 5	St. Cloud, MN	**9th Bike Service (39,700 miles) oils**
43	Sunday, July 6	Butte, MT	
44	Monday, July 7	Watertown, SD	
45	Tuesday, July 8	Belgrade, MT	
46	Wednesday, July 9	Lincoln, NE	
47	Thursday, July 10	St. Cloud, MN	**10th Bike Service (44,900 miles) oils/tires**
48	Friday, July 11	Butte, MT	
49	Saturday, July 12	Watertown, SD	
50	Sunday, July 13	Belgrade, MT	
51	Monday, July 14	Lincoln, NE	**11th Bike Service (50,100 miles) oils**
52	Tuesday, July 15	St. Cloud, MN	**6th Bike Service (53,940 miles)**
53	Wednesday, July 16	Butte, MT	
54	Thursday, July 17	Watertown, SD	
55	Friday, July 18	Belgrade, MT	

NO BOUNDARIES TOUR

56	Saturday, July 19	Lincoln, NE	
57	Sunday, July 20	St. Cloud, MN	**12th Bike Service (55,300 miles) oils**
58	Monday, July 21	Butte, MT	
59	Tuesday, July 22	Watertown, SD	
60	Wednesday, July 23	Belgrade, MT	
61	Thursday, July 24	Lincoln, NE	
62	Friday, July 25	St. Cloud, MN	**13th Bike Service (60,500 miles) oils/tires**
63	Saturday, July 26	Butte, MT	
64	Sunday, July 27	Watertown, SD	
65	Monday, July 28	Belgrade, MT	
66	Tuesday, July 29	Lincoln, NE	
67	Wednesday, July 30	St. Cloud, MN	**14th Bike Service (65,700 miles) oils**
68	Thursday, July 31	Butte, MT	
69	Friday, Aug. 1	Watertown, SD	
70	Saturday, Aug. 2	Belgrade, MT	
71	Sunday, Aug. 3	Lincoln, NE	
72	Monday, Aug. 4	St. Cloud, MN	**15th Bike Service (70,900 miles) oils**
73	Tuesday, Aug. 5	Butte, MT	**85th Sturgis, SD Rally "Meet & Greet***
74	Wednesday, Aug. 6	Watertown, SD	
75	Thursday, Aug. 7	Belgrade, MT	
76	Friday, Aug. 8	Lincoln, NE	

77	Saturday, Aug. 9	St. Cloud, MN	**16th Bike Service (76,100 miles) oils/tires**
78	Sunday, Aug. 10	Butte, MT	
79	Monday, Aug. 11	Watertown, SD	**85th Sturgis, SD Rally "Meet & Greet"**
80	Tuesday, Aug. 12	Belgrade, MT	
81	Wednesday, Aug. 13	Lincoln, NE	
82	Thursday, Aug. 14	St. Cloud, MN	**17th Bike Service (81,300 miles) oils**
83	Friday, Aug. 15	Butte, MT	
84	Saturday, Aug. 16	Watertown, SD	
85	Sunday, Aug. 17	Belgrade, MT	
86	Monday, Aug. 18	Lincoln, NE	
87	Tuesday, Aug. 19	St. Cloud, MN	**18th Bike Service (86,500 miles) oils**
88	Wednesday, Aug. 20	Butte, MT	
89	Thursday, Aug. 21	Watertown, SD	
90	Friday, Aug. 22	Belgrade, MT	
91	Saturday, Aug. 23	Lincoln, NE	
92	Sunday, Aug. 24	St. Cloud, MN	**19th Bike Service (91,700 miles) oils/tires**
93	Monday, Aug. 25	Butte, MT	
94	Tuesday, Aug. 26	Watertown, SD	
95	Wednesday, Aug. 27	Belgrade, MT	

96	Thursday, Aug. 28	Lincoln, NE	
97	Friday, Aug. 29	St. Cloud, MN	**20th Bike Service (96,900 miles) oils**
98	Saturday, Aug. 30	Butte, MT	
99	Sunday, Aug. 31	Watertown, SD	
100	Monday, Sept. 1	Belgrade, MT	Holiday
101	Tuesday, Sept. 2	Lincoln, NE	
102	Wednesday, Sept. 3	St. Cloud, MN	**21st Bike Service (102,100 miles) oils**
103	Thursday, Sept. 4	Butte, MT	
104	Friday, Sept. 5	Watertown, SD	
105	Saturday, Sept. 6	Belgrade, MT	
106	Sunday, Sept. 7	Lincoln, NE	
107	Monday, Sept. 8	St. Cloud, MN	**22nd Bike Service (107,300 miles) oils/tires**
108	Tuesday, Sept. 9	Butte, MT	
109	Wednesday, Sept. 10	Watertown, SD	
110	Thursday, Sept. 11	Belgrade, MT	
111	Friday, Sept. 12	Lincoln, NE	
112	Saturday, Sept. 13	St. Cloud, MN	**23rd Bike Service (112,500 miles) oils**
113	Sunday, Sept. 14	Butte, MT	
114	Monday, Sept. 15	Watertown, SD	
115	Tuesday, Sept. 16	Belgrade, MT	

116	Wednesday, Sept. 17	Lincoln, NE	
117	Thursday, Sept. 18	St. Cloud, MN	**24th Bike Service (120,000 miles) oils/tires**
118	Saturday, Sept. 20	Viking Land HD St. Cloud, MN	Celebration

80 (Midweek days) / 3 (HOLIDAYS) / 34 (WEEKEND Days) = 117 Total Days (17 Weeks Total)

Motels:

- Butte, MT - 23 nights
- Watertown, SD - 23 nights
- Belgrade, MT - 23 nights
- Lincoln, NE - 23 nights
- St. Cloud, MN - 24 nights
- Louisville, KY - 1 night

Harley-Davidson Dealers (17 Dealers in 7 States):

1	Viking Land HD3555	Shadowwood Dr. NE, St. Cloud, MN	320-251-6980
2	Apols HD1515	42nd Ave W, Alexandria, MN	320-763-9800
3	HD of Fargo701	Christianson Dr., West Fargo, ND	701-277-1000
4	Stutsman HD2501	3rd Ave SW, Jamestown, ND	701-252-5271
5	Beartooth HD6900	S Frontage Rd., Billings, MT	406-252-2888
6	Yellowstone HD540	Alaska Frontage Rd., Belgrade, MT	406-388-7684

7	Copper Canyon HD34	Olympic Way, Butte, MT	406-782-5601
8	DeluxeHD3300	Conestoga Dr., Gillette, WY	307-687-2001
9	High Country HD3320	E Lincolnway, Cheyenne, WY	307-638-8307
10	Black Hills HD2820	Harley Dr., Rapid City, SD	605-342-9362
11	J&L HD2601	W 60th St N., Sioux Falls, SD	605-334-2721
12	Glacial Lakes HD1000	19th St SE, Watertown, SD	605-886-3448
13	Frontier HD205	NW 40th St., Lincoln, NE	402-466-9100
14	Defiance HD4940	S 72nd St., Omaha, NE	402-331-0022
15	Dillon Brothers HD3838	N HWS Cleveland Blvd., Omaha, NE	402-289-5556
16	Roosters HD1930	N Lewis Blvd., Sioux City, IA	712-252-2750
17	Rough Rider HD3708	Memorial Hwy., Mandan, ND	701-663-2220

Sponsorship Letter Example
TO: Potential Partners for World Record Setting Motorcycle Charity Ride

LOCATED: Continuous 120,000-mile rotation route that includes the fifteen states of Florida, Georgia, Tennessee, Kentucky, Indiana, Illinois, Iowa, Minnesota, North Dakota, Montana, Wyoming, South Dakota, Nebraska, Missouri, and Wisconsin.

FROM: Scott Gottschalk
73078 CSAH 19
Kimball, MN. 55353
320-894-5900
GottschalkScott@yahoo.com

DURATION: May 25 to September 18, 2025 (120,000 miles in 120 continuous days of riding)

SUBJECT: World Record Motorcycle Ride Charity Fundraiser: No Boundaries Tour, The Fight Against Human Trafficking

120th Anniversary HD Motorcycle, covering **120,000 miles** in **120 days** of continuous +1,000 miles per day completed by one rider on one motorcycle.

Proposal: Sponsorship/Partnership with You

Thank you for taking the time to consider this opportunity. It was fun discussing some of the pre-planning actions vital for a 2025 attempt to set a new motorcycle distance world record. If successful, that would establish a new world record for the most total miles driven, for the most consecutive days, with the same rider, and on the same motorcycle, all while fundraising for a noble cause to help others with difficult and unbearable hardships. Certainly, this would not be a motorcycle ride for the faint of heart since the physical, mental, mechanical, and financial demands for both man and machine are simply astonishing. If accomplished, however, that would then become a legendary achievement and become a lifelong memory for all who were involved in such a noble endeavor!

    I've provided you and/or your organization with as much of the details as I'm able to describe at this juncture of planning for this world record attempt during the summer of 2025. The main reason I wanted to contact you as a possible sponsor lies in the fact that during my 120-day riding rotation to cover 120,000 miles, you and/or your team could be a supporter of this cause. During this ride, I will literally travel near your location sometime during the duration of the 120-day event. In fact, during that year, the Sturgis Bike Rally will also celebrate its 85th Anniversary, so imagine the "Meet and Greet Promotions" possible while I'm traveling along the designated route. This trip could garner some amazing national and international PR, along with sales and marketing opportunities should you choose to participate with some level of sponsorship.

Please discuss this proposal with your key team members to discuss this sponsorship notion. I'm excited to listen to some of your ideas for success and implementation of this ride.

As I'd mentioned to you, I've been fortunate to hold many motorcycling long-distance riding achievements. Over the decades, I've established a new world record by certifying a +10,000-mile ride that covered all 48 Continental US states in just over 6.5 days on my 110-year Anniversary Model 2013 HD Ultra-Limited. Over the years, beginning with my 90-year Anniversary Model 1993 HD Springer-Softail, I've logged more than 70 rides of 1,000 mile in less than 24 hours, I've logged more than 30 rides of 1,500 miles in less than 24 hours, and I've completed a "Border to Border Insanity Ride" of nearly 1,600 miles from Canada into Mexico in less than 24 hours while riding on my 100-year Anniversary 2003 HD Ultra-Classic. I've also certified rides of 2,000 miles in under 32 hours, along with certified a 10/10th Ride by riding ten, 1,000-mile days consecutively all around the outside edges of the United States. In addition, I'm also the only rider to certify a 1,500-mile ride in under 24 hours by riding an old-school custom-built HD hard-tail chopper with no suspension. (FYI, that was a bit hard on my body!)

This is by no means my entire long-distance motorcycle riding résumé, but hopefully, this info does lend itself toward some credibility for my riding abilities and endurance levels.

Some key elements of this ride sponsorship:

- Ride will be completed with a new 120-year Anniversary Model 2023 HD FLTRK Road Glide Limited, prospect gold/black w/ black trim purchased by me at retail.
- Financial support for maintenance/service/parts requiring up to 12 full tires changes and 24 full-service intervals over the entire 120,000-mile journey.
- If this world record is set, then consideration for displaying the "tougher-than-nails" 2023 Harley-Davidson World Record Holding Motorcycle at one of your future "Appreciation Events" will be anticipated.
- Keynote motivational speaking presentations and talks for various meetings, business conferences, and events. **I'm a long-standing professional speaker that provides enthusiastic and passionate keynote talks.
- The goal will be to complete this world record ride as I celebrate my 70th birthday!

Please reach out to me with your thoughts, and thank you so much for your consideration. I look forward to hearing from you.

Scott Gottschalk
73078 CSAH 19
Kimball, Minnesota 55353
320-895-5900
GottschalkScott@Yahoo.com

CHAPTER 8
No Boundaries Tour Presentation

The Bike --- 2023 FLTRK Road Glide Limited
120th Anniversary Harley Davidson

@ NoBoundariesTour.com

My Belief

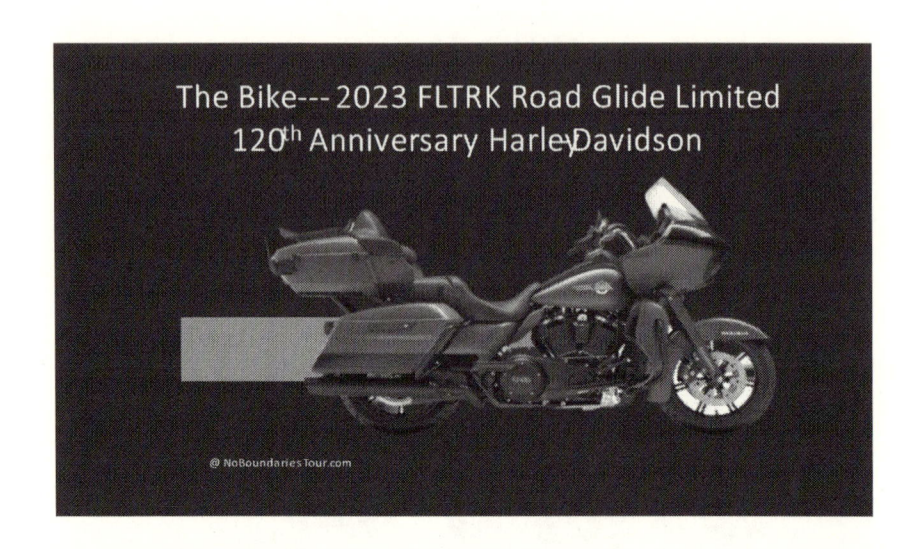

Life is made up of two dates and a dash, make the most of the dash.

" I have come to realize that I may not be right in the head, however I am completely fine with that idea."
- Scott Gottschalk

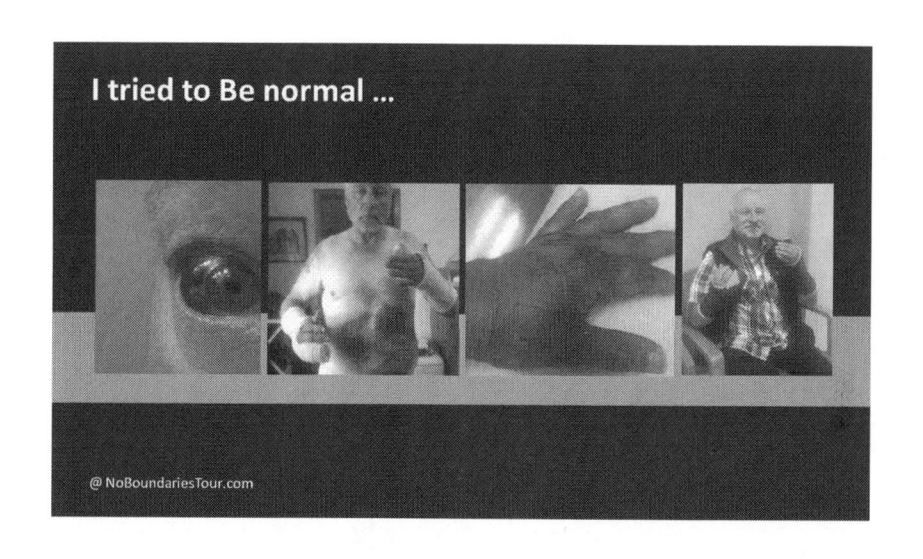

NO BOUNDARIES TOUR

I tried to Be normal ...

@ NoBoundariesTour.com

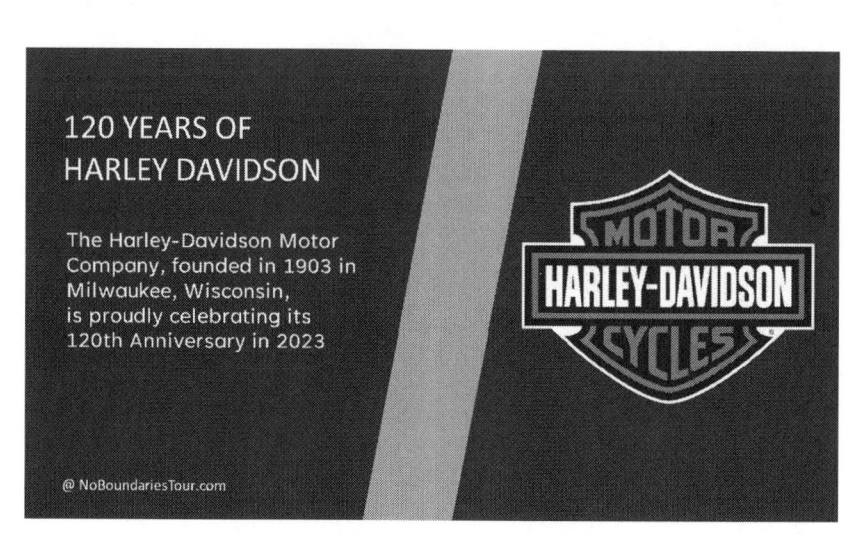

120 YEARS OF
HARLEY DAVIDSON

The Harley-Davidson Motor
Company, founded in 1903 in
Milwaukee, Wisconsin,
is proudly celebrating its
120th Anniversary in 2023

HARLEY-DAVIDSON
MOTOR CYCLES

@ NoBoundariesTour.com

SCOTT D. GOTTSCHALK

GOAL Ride 120,000 Miles in 120 Days
Nearly 5 Times around the Circumference of the entire World !

Main goal is to focus on experience and images and show people the world from various perspectives.

@ NoBoundariesTour.com

Guinness Book

Each record title must fulfill all of the following criteria. They must be:

Measurable
Breakable
Standardizable
Verifiable based on one variable
The best in the world

BREAKING the RECORD:
The longest journey by motorcycle in a single country (individual)

@ NoBoundariesTour.com

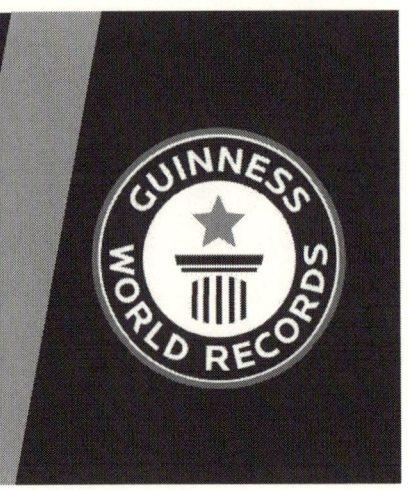

NO BOUNDARIES TOUR

IRON BUTT

IBA Riding Tips

The 82,000+ members of the Iron Butt Association are dedicated to safe, long-distance motorcycle riding.

@ NoBoundariesTour.com

World's Toughest Motorcycle Riders — Iron Butt Association

The Details

120,000 miles in under 120 days of continuous +1,000 miles per day riding/same rider/same HD motorcycle

DURATION: May 23 to September 16, 2025
120,564 miles in 120 continuous days riding

SUBJECT: World Record Motorcycle Charity Ride:
"Stop Human Trafficking"

@ NoBoundariesTour.com

SCOTT D. GOTTSCHALK

The Details

- A new, never-ridden (120-year Anniversary Model) 2023 FLTRK Road Glide Limited

- Keynote Motivational Speaking presentations and talks for various meetings, business conferences, and events. I'm a long-standing professional speaker that provides enthusiastic and passionate keynote talks.

- The goal will be to complete this World Record ride on September 16, 2025, to celebrate my 70th Birthday Party on that exact day!

@ NoBoundariesTour.com

Continuous 5-day rotation

*1st Day of rotation:	Night in Kingston, MN	(16+ hours)	1,025 miles
*2nd Day of rotation:	Night in Butte, MT	(16+ hours)	1,008 miles
*3rd Day of rotation:	Night in Watertown, SD	(16+ hours)	1,060 miles
*4th Day of rotation:	Night in Bozeman, MT	(16+ hours)	1,050 miles
*5th Day of rotation:	Night in Lincoln, NE	(16+ hours)	1,005 miles

TOTAL MILES IN 5-Day ROTATION   (1030-mile average per day):   5,150 miles

@ NoBoundariesTour.com

NO BOUNDARIES TOUR

ROUTE

Route:
1000+ miles a day for 120 days

Total Days

1030-mile average per day:

- May 23-31, 2025   9 days
- June 1-30, 2025   30 days
- July 1-31, 2025   31 days
- August 1-31, 2025   31 days
- September 1-16, 2025 (Scott Gottschalk 70th Birthday 9/16/25!)   16 days

*TOTAL Proposed Continuous Riding Days To Complete: 120 days

@ NoBoundariesTour.com

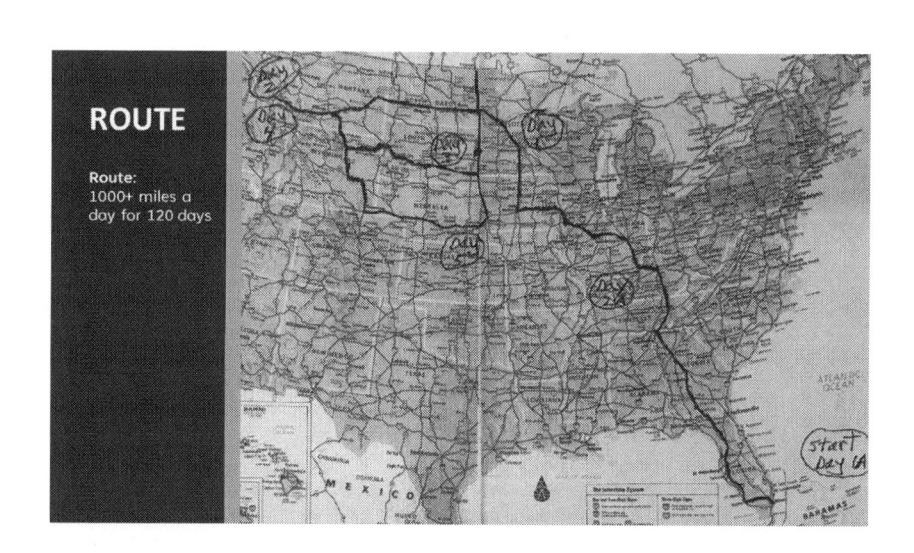

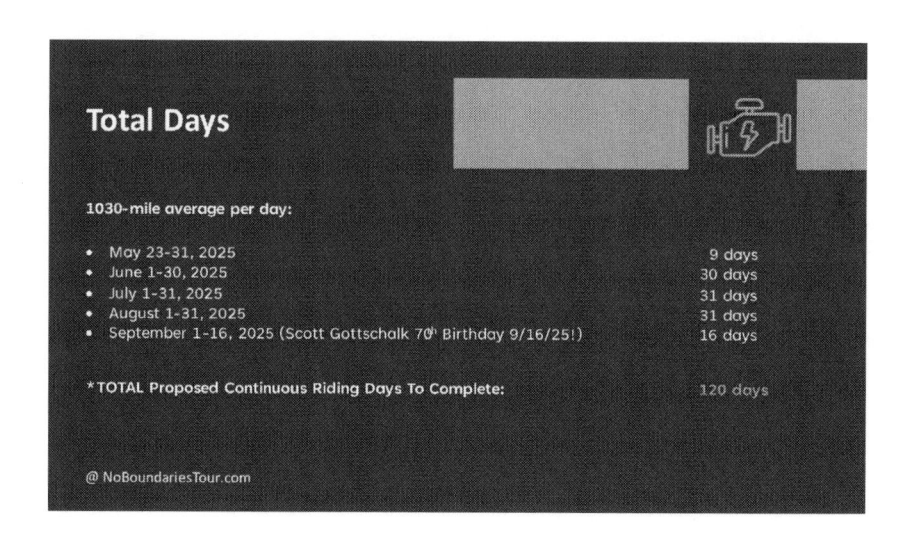

RIDE SPECIFICS

- 12 full tire changes
- 12 oil changes & service
- 94 motel nights
- 23 nights at home
- 120 days food
- 120 days X 1,030 mi/day X 65 mph Ave (+16 hours/day) riding = 120,500 total miles
- 120,000 miles @ 40 mpg (5 gal. tank) = 3,000 gal (+600 total fills)
- 24 months of preparation
- 5 days of pre-ride
- Extensive pre-ride nutritional and physical workout regime
- 1000 days marketing

APPROXIMATE TOUR COSTS = $125,000

@ NoBoundariesTour.com

RULES of the road

Route:
1000+ miles a day for 120 days

Beta Journey / Test Run:
5 days April 30 – May 4, 2023

Detour Strategy
Zoom Check-in
Tracking System
Speed Limits
Ride-A-Longs
Health Stress Monitoring
Safety Parameters
Weather Challenges
Mechanical Maintenance
Mindset
Physical Endurance Preparation

@ NoBoundariesTour.com

NO BOUNDARIES TOUR

MATERIALS

Brand Logo / Guide
Website & Domain Name
Social Media
Press Release
Documentary
GoFundMe.com
Merchandising
Promo Videos
Posters
Wearables
QR Code
Launch Event

@ NoBoundariesTour.com

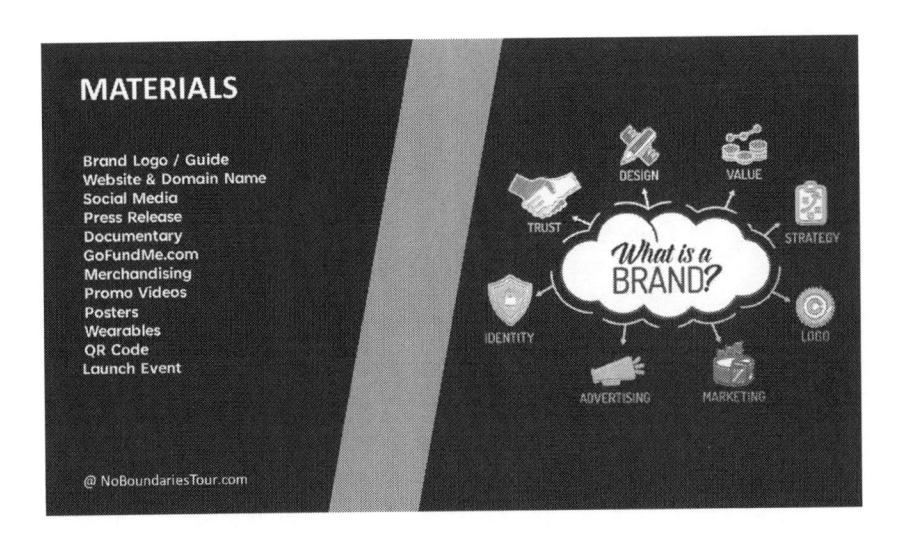

MOTIVATIONAL MISSIONS

Motivational Missions Strives to be the Catalyst of Positive Youth Development

Motivational Missions (MMT) is 501(C)3 non-profit, non-religious organization designed to help children around the world through educational seminars and media awareness campaigns.

Proceeds from the tour will Benefit this org.

Campaigns Include: Prevention of Human Trafficking

www.MMtour.org
#CauseWeCare

HUMAN TRAFFICKING ROUTES

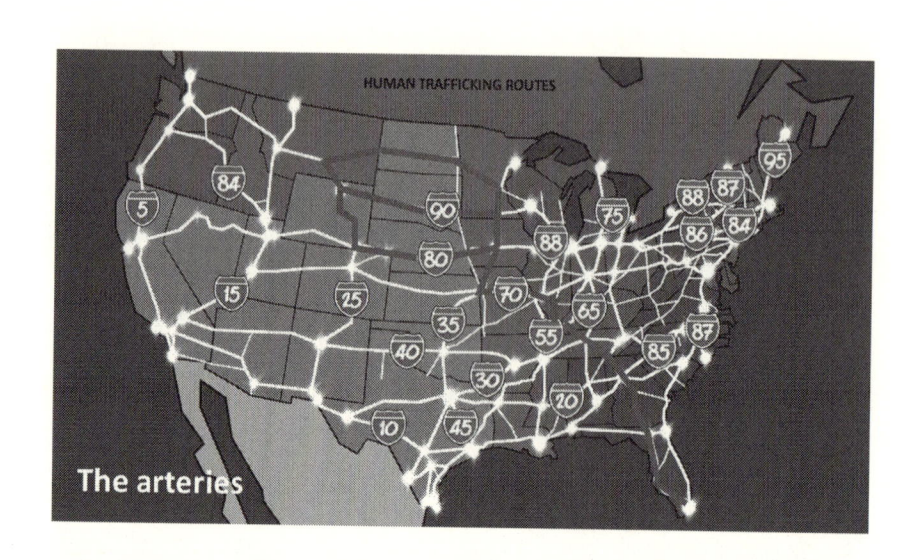

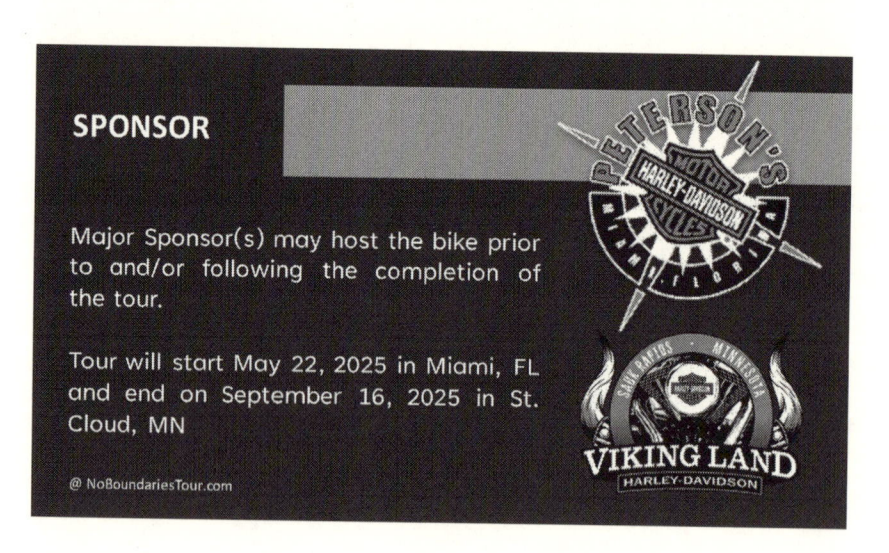

The arteries

SPONSOR

Major Sponsor(s) may host the bike prior to and/or following the completion of the tour.

Tour will start May 22, 2025 in Miami, FL and end on September 16, 2025 in St. Cloud, MN

@ NoBoundariesTour.com

PETERSON'S HARLEY-DAVIDSON MOTORCYCLES

VIKING LAND HARLEY-DAVIDSON

We only regret the rides we did not take...

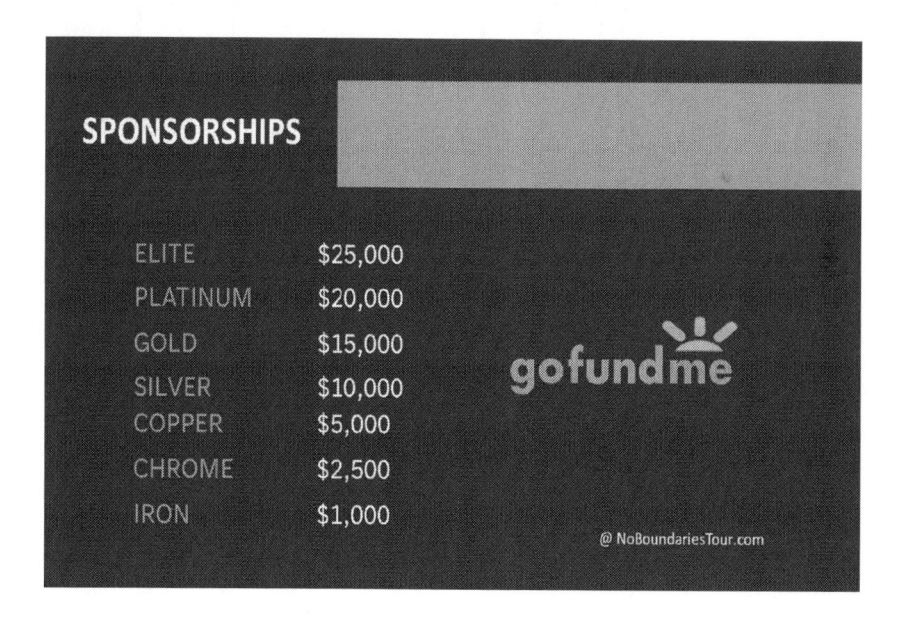

@ NoBoundariesTour.com

SPONSORSHIPS

ELITE	$25,000
PLATINUM	$20,000
GOLD	$15,000
SILVER	$10,000
COPPER	$5,000
CHROME	$2,500
IRON	$1,000

gofundme

@ NoBoundariesTour.com

CHAPTER 9
Sponsorships and Press Release

SCOTT D. GOTTSCHALK

No Boundaries Tour

SPONSORSHIPS
2025

POWERED BY: BOWA STUDIOS

@NoBoundariesTour | www.NoBoundariesTour.com

NO BOUNDARIES TOUR
120,000 MILES

THE HARLEY-DAVIDSON MOTOR COMPANY, FOUNDED IN 1903 IN MILWAUKEE, WISCONSIN, IS PROUDLY CELEBRATING ITS 120TH ANNIVERSARY IN 2023

Mr. Scott Gottschalk is going to have the ride of his life and enter into the Guinness World Book of Records. He will be riding 120,000 miles in 120 days on a 120 Anniversary Harley Davidson.

Challenge Information:

Bike: Brand New 2023 FLT Road Glide Special Edition [Already in Possession]

Trip: 120,000 miles in under 120 days of continuous +1,000 miles per day riding/same rider/same HD motorcycle

Proposed Dates: May 23 to September 18, 2025 (120,564 miles in 120 continuous days riding)

Goal: Set a World Record Motorcycle Ride 4 Others to: "Stop Human Trafficking"

1030 mile average per day):   5,150 miles**

- May 23-31, 2025   9 days
- June 1-30, 2025   30 days
- July 1-31, 2025   31 days
- August 1-31, 2025   31 days
- September 1-18, 2025 (Scott Gottschalk 70th Birthday 9/16/25!)   18 days

*TOTAL Proposed Continuous Riding Days To Complete: 120 days

Route: 1000+ miles a day for 120 days
Beta Journey / Test Run: 5 days May 1-5, 2023

ROAD RULES
Detour Strategy	Health Stress Monitoring
Zoom Check-in	Safety Parameters
Tracking System	Weather Challenges
Speed Limits	Mechanical Maintenance
Ride A Longs	Mindset

@NoBoundariesTour | www.NoBoundariesTour.com

SCOTT D. GOTTSCHALK

TOUR HIGHLIGHTS & MAIN GOAL

Scott Gottschalk

Main Goal is to focus on the experience and show people the world from various perspectives.

INTERNATIONAL SPEAKER
Scott was not only an Agriculture Education Instructor, but for more than thirty years he has served as an International Consultant. He has globetrotted across all seven continents, including Antarctica, and more than forty countries, providing services in exotic locations such as Siberian Russia, Uganda, Lebanon, and Afghanistan.

Scott G Website: www.ScottDGottschalk.com

CAPTIVATING AUTHOR
Experienced in live audience communications, he has captivated audiences across our planet with his motivational and passionate inspirational messages. He has written three books including, THE FOLK AND THEIR FAUNA, NINE LIVES TO ETERNITY, and TERRIFYING TALES UNLEASHED.

Proceeds from this tour will benefit this organization.

Motivational Missions Strives to be the Catalyst of a Positive Youth Development Motivational Missions (MMT) is 501(C)3 non-profit, non-religious organization designed to help children around the world through, educational seminars and media awareness campaigns.

We will be registering this tour to the Guinness World Book of Records.

BREAKING the RECORD:
The longest journey by motorcycle in a single country (individual)

We will be registering this tour to the:

The 82,000+ members of the Iron Butt Association are dedicated to safe, long-distance motorcycle riding.

NO BOUNDARIES TOUR

SPONSOR LEVELS
LAUNCHING 2025

Sponsorships Include:	Routes Sponsor	Rally Sponsor	Baggers Sponsors	Interstate Sponsors
CSR- Corporate Social Responsibility	$240,000	$120,000	$60,000	$30,000
Available Spots	1 Spot	3 Spots	5 Spots	10 Spots
Invitations to Send Off Party Night	10	8	6	4
Logo on Website	✓	✓	✓	✓
Logo on Sponsor Thank You PPT	✓	✓	✓	✓
Giveaways at Launch*	✓	✓	✓	✓
Logo on Launch Video	✓	✓	✓	✓
Logo on Support Trailer/Vehicle	3'x3'	2'x2'	1'x1'	
Logo on Tour Tent	✓	✓		
Sponsor Banners at Event*	✓	✓		
Start Line Banner	✓	✓		
Finish Line Banner	✓	✓		
Step/Repeat Banner	✓	✓		
Logo on Tour Motorcycle	✓			
Tour T-Shirt Logo	✓			
2:00 Speech on Stage at Launch	✓			
Podcast Interview	✓			
Mentions in Press Announcements	✓			
Logo on Recap Video	✓			
Keynote Speech by Scott Gottschalk	✓			
Logo on Commemorative Poker Chip	✓			
Book Dedication	✓			

*Must be provided by sponsor.

UNLIMITED DONATION LEVELS	Support Level	Ride with Scott*	NBT Patch	Website Mention	Book Mention
Rough Rider	$10,000	5,000 miles	✓	✓	✓
Easy Rider	$5,000	1000 miles	✓	✓	✓

*Rider must comply with all NBT rules and regulations.

@NoBoundariesTour | www.NoBoundariesTour.com

177

SPONSOR AGREEMENT FORM

Name _____ Date _____

Company _____ Title _____

Address _____ City _____

State _____ Zip Code _____

Cell Phone _____ Email _____

Contact Person _____ Phone _____

Event Name: LAUNCH PARTY in Miami, FL

Date: Saturday – May 24, 2025   Start Time: 4:00pm   End Time: 8:00pm

Please indicate which level you will be committing to:

Routes Sponsor	Rally Sponsor	Baggers Sponsors	Interstate Sponsors
$240,000	$120,000	$60,000	$30,000

DONOR LEVELS:

- ☐ Harley $ 7,500
- ☐ Iron Butt $ 5,000
- ☐ Guinness $ 2,500
- ☐ Highway $ 1,000
- ☐ Ride Patches $ _____
- ☐ Other $ _____

Total: $ _____ USD

Method of Payment:

- ☐ Check #_____ (Payable to Motivational Missions)
- ☐ Credit Card _____

Credit Card No: ___ ___ ___ ___   EXP: _____   CVV: _____

Name on Card: _____   Signature: _____

MotivationalMissions.org
13501 SW 128 Street Ste 212
Miami, FL 33186

PRESS RELEASE
No Boundaries Tour 2025

Announces a World Record Motorcycle Ride to Stop Human Trafficking

Miami, Florida / Kimball, Minnesota (May 2025) – The Motivational Missions nonprofit company is proud to announce its sponsorship of the **No Boundaries Tour 2025**, a 120,000-mile ride on a brand new 2023 FLT Road Glide Limited motorcycle, aimed at setting a world record for the longest journey by motorcycle in a single country (individual) and raising awareness and funds to stop human trafficking.

The **No Boundaries Tour 2025** will be powered by Scott Gottschalk, an international speaker and captivating author, who has globetrotted across all seven continents, including Antarctica, and more than seventy countries, providing services in exotic locations such as Siberian Russia, Uganda, Lebanon, and Afghanistan. Scott will embark on this epic journey from May 25, 2025, to September 18, 2025, covering 120,564 miles in 120 continuous days of riding. The official launch will be at Peterson's Harley Davidson in Cutler Bay (Miami, Florida) on Saturday, May 24, 2025, from 4:00 to 8:00 p.m.

The **No Boundaries Tour 2025** will have a detour strategy, zoom check-ins, tracking system, speed limits, ride-alongs, health stress monitoring, safety parameters, weather challenges, mechanical maintenance, and mindset to ensure the success of the trip. The tour had a beta journey / test run of 5,180 miles over the course of 5 days from April 30 to May 4, 2023.

Proceeds from this tour will benefit **Motivational Missions**, a 501(C)3 nonprofit, nonreligious organization designed to help children around the world through educational seminars and local, national, and international media awareness campaigns to raise awareness of human trafficking.

"We are thrilled to sponsor the **No Boundaries Tour 2025** and support Scott an international dairy consultant / farmer, in his mission to set a world record by his 70th birthday, and raise awareness and funds to stop human trafficking," said Alexa Oliva, founder of Motivational Missions. "MMT has always stood for making an impact and informing our communities, and we believe that Scott's journey embodies these values."

The tour will register for the Guinness World Book of Records and the 82,000+ members of the Iron Butt Association, dedicated to safe long-distance motorcycle riding.

For more information, please visit www.NoBoundariesTour.com and http://www.NBTRide.com.

Media Contact: Valerie Leichtman (954) 691-5505 (val@mmtour.org)

CHAPTER 10
Pre-Ride Practice (We Can Do This!)

Questions asked of myself, repeatedly, "If we think we can do this, then first we must practice. Are we tough enough?" "Can the body hold up under the endless hours of physical and mental torment?" "Will the machine hold up under such endless perturbing hours and the extreme milage conditions for the better part of 18 hours per day for 120 straight days in a row?" "Can man and machine actually accomplish such a feat?"

The immense pre-planning to undertake or to even fathom attempting to break a World Record Motorcycle Charity Ride of this magnitude would stop most humans dead in their tracks. Perhaps only a minuscule few common humans with uncommon dreams and ambitions can perceive and ultimately reach such unimaginable performances of the human spirit.

For this specific Motorcycling Distance World Record attempt to start off on the intended month and year of May 2025, I'd began the initial thought processes four years prior in 2021. My competitive juices surged immediately following the announcement of a major Long-Distance Iron Butt Association Motorcycling World Record set by a fellow long-distance colleague biker.

At the writing of this book, the current distance-ride world record was established for the Iron Butt Association (IBA) Long-Distance Motorcycle Riding World Record. This record was dubbed the "Saddle Sore 100,000" and covered

100,454 miles in 100 consecutive days of riding through all 48 contiguous states. This record shattered the previous legendary long-distance rider Matt Wise's 45,000 miles in 45 days IBA World Record. That remarkable current world record was achieved by Chris Hopper from Texas whose ride went from July 27 to November 4, 2021, riding on his 2021 Harley-Davidson Road Glide Limited motorcycle. Not only did Chris set the new motorcycle distance record, but he also raised more than $100,000 to benefit those with Duchenne Muscular Dystrophy (DMD), a genetic disorder that causes progressive muscle degeneration, usually among young boys.

My utmost esteem and respect will always be there toward Chris Hopper for setting a new legendary motorcycling milage mark that will be an arduous challenge for anyone to set a higher mark!

With the knowledge in my mind that someone out there had logged such an immense total of miles on a motorcycle while doing it for a noble charity fundraiser, I commenced preplanning a personal route for my own motorcycle ride record attempt that could possibly set a new IBA Record. I initially set my IBA World Record milage attempt at 110,000 miles in 110 days.

I'm an extremely compulsive-personality type, so I "kick-started" my way of thinking and began route planning for nearly a full year from 2021 through 2022 when another motorcycling world record milestone was attained and announced.

At the writing of this book, the current Guiness Book of World Records ride for the longest journey by motorcycle in a single country (individual) was achieved from April 3 to August 5, 2022, by Dana D'Arcy. She rode her 2020 Harley-Davidson Road Glide Limited motorcycle an incredible 82,598 miles in 125 days. Dana took a four-month sabbatical from her career as a certified registered nurse anesthetist in South Florida to experience her once-in-a-lifetime motorcycle trip. She averaged over 660 miles per day and only missed two days of riding the entire time due to a shredded drive belt.

My utmost admiration and reverence will always be there toward Dana D'Arcy for taking the time to fill out the extensive Guiness Book of World Records Application form and then reaching the stringent Guiness World Record criteria to earn her fabled motorcycling milage mark that will be an arduous challenge for anyone to surpass!

My competitive urges flowed even further as I contemplated bridging the two motorcycling records into one. My first instincts were that I'm a certified Iron Butt Association member in good standing, so therefore I was only initially interested in trying for the IBA world record. Because of input from friends and other long-distance motorcycle riders, the concept of also completing a Guiness Book of World Records application did have some merits. My argument was I only cared about the IBA record that other long-distance motorcycle enthusiasts adhere to. The converse argument was that more people worldwide were aware of the Guiness Book of World Record achievements than that of the motorcycle Iron Butt Association records.

It was then I had an epiphany in late 2022, as I proceeded ahead with the plan to combine both the Guiness World Record and the IBA world record, and thus I reset my record ride criteria targeting 120,000 miles, within 120 days, while attempting to raise $1.2 million dollars to "fight human trafficking and sexual exploitation." This I would attempt to achieve while riding on my personally full-retail-purchased 120th Anniversary Harley-Davidson 2023 HD Road Glide Limited motorcycle. Our No Boundaries Tour Ride for Charity forecasting unveiled a course for a May through September 2025 120-day run, traveling +1000 miles per day route that followed along many of the main "human trafficking" interstate highway routes across a fifteen-state route, albeit mainly a seven-state route inside the United States of America highways.

First things first, we held a Gottschalk family meeting in 2022, a full three years before my perceived motorcycle record attempt. That meeting consisted of my wife, Astrid; our eldest son, Trevor; and his wife, Theresa; along with our youngest son, Travis; and his wife, RaeLynn. In that family meeting, I detailed my thoughts to combine the Guiness and Iron Butt Association motorcycle distance world records. That concept was met with little enthusiasm from anyone within my family.

As I've spelled out in earlier chapters of this book, my family and my friends have witnessed some horrendous motorcycling accidents, resulting in severe physical injuries from some of my extreme motorcycling rides in the past.

As an outcome of our joint family meetings, my loving and deeply caring family generally and mutually agreed to support me in my escapades of extreme motorcycling, and they surmise to support me as I put all my passion and efforts toward achieving the end goal; however, every one of my family members sincerely wish that I would discontinue taking on such extreme risks. Risks that may put me in harm's way once again or, even worse yet, possibly end my existence on this planet.

With family matters settled, I thought, I began planning my continuous +5,180-mile motorcycling route. A path canvasing a semicircular seven-state track that I could pre-ride and then submit to the Iron Butt Association as an official pre-qualifying IBA Saddle Sore 5,000 (+1,000 miles per day for five days). If accepted, then my expectation was to ride that same route or a few variations of it repeatedly until the defined +120,000 miles world record would fall. So with all the GPS coordinates mapped out, all the twists and turns along the +5,000 miles route determined, along with all the fuel stops, nightly motel stops, and maintenance needs pre-identified, I was all set to complete my "pre-ride practice run" that took place on May 1, 2, 3, 4, 5, 2023.

It sure verbally sounded great and even looked prodigious on paper, but on May 1, 2022, the hard, cold reality of the real deal was about to set forth for this kind of undertaking.

Pre-Ride Day 1: 4:00 a.m., Monday, May 1, 2023. Outside temperature is a balmy low of 30 degrees Fahrenheit. May 1 in rural Minnesota at 3:00 a.m. is very dark and a tad bit chilly to begin a +5,000-mile, five-day, nonstop motorcycle journey. This being my first motorcycle ride of this year, I know better than to simply hop on a motorcycle that has been idle all Minnesota winter long, but I've mentioned before, I'm a rather compulsive individual at times. I've done enough long-distance motorcycle rides to know it is best for one to be in riding shape, and one should already have logged a bunch of miles on a motorcycle before hopping on for the first time during a new riding season, and then hoping to ride five, +1,000-mile days consecutively.

No matter, I convinced myself that I was tough enough even at my active age of 67 years to complete my mission. I've done this many times before, what's the big deal that I didn't get my body prepared this time. It's only a five-day ride, right?

The cold outside temperatures kept my Harley-Davidson 110th Year Harley-Davidson 2013 Electra Glide Ultra-Limited motorcycle well below its typical engine operating temperatures while waiting for the sun to peek over the horizon warming both man and machine up a bit.

My motorcycle was traveling along at the posted 70 mph speed limit along Interstate 94 North through Minnesota onwards toward North Dakota. Once I reached North Dakota, the posted limit increased to 75 mph speed limit thus became the norm. I would typically stop for a fuel stop between every 150–175 miles. I knew that "Big-Twin" engine Harley's fuel efficiency drops substantially whenever pushing them at higher RPMs and higher highway speeds, but I needed to keep the pace to stay on an 18-hour-or-under daily time constraint.

As I passed along I-94 through the aftermath of a massive, late-season snowstorm, my bike and I traveled past 15-foot-tall snowbanks. I whisked by plowed-out portions of snowdrifts that had made a pathway through the Interstate Highway System of North Dakota, and it was May 1. I sure hope the wintertime extremes will soon be over!

After traveling more than 12 hours, I hit the high plains dessert area of Montana and the daytime temps had by then crawled up to over 80 degrees Fahrenheit. With a +50 degree swing in temps within 12 hours, I'd gone from frozen fingers and chattering teeth to stripping off some layers of clothes while still sweating profusely. During the early morning, my motorcycle had struggled to reach proper engine operating temps, but now my engine temperature gauge reflected my engine was overheating as I maintained the present Montana posted 80 mph interstate highway speed limit, all while starting to climb up some very steep Rocky Mountain grades of highway.

With less than two hours left to roll on day one and at the top of a Montana Interstate 94 mountain pass, my motorcycle finally got too hot while pushing it so hard up one mountain grade after another. With a massive backfire, I watched oil start pouring from the engine air intake and saw my engine oil pressure gauge drop to nearly zero. I pulled onto the Interstate I-94 shoulder and watched about two quarts of oil flow nonstop from the right side of my machine due to the massive back pressure that had built up inside my engine and transmission. I pulled my oil dipstick only to find that the oil in my engine was no longer reaching the very bottom of the dipstick.

In a panic, and thankfully finally accessing a cell phone signal where I'd had none before that point, I made a call to Ron Hugit in Litchfield, Minnesota, who is one of my dearest friends and my personal motorcycle mechanic. I needed to get some mechanical opinion from Ron on what he thought had happened and what I should to do about it to get back on the road. Ron determined that I was likely pushing too many RPMs up steep mountain grades causing my bike to rebel. I'll admit, I was making her work hard to maintain a cruising speed of 80 mph. He suggested that I put my two spare quarts of oil, which I'd packed in my saddlebags into the bike to top it off again, and then drive more conservatively until reaching my nighttime destination waiting up ahead in Butte, Montana.

I made it that short trek without further mechanical incident into Butte, Montana, just prior to nightfall at about 9:00 p.m. Thankfully, mechanically my motorcycle never acted up again during its +5,000-mile pre-ride. With the remaining daylight, on day one, I rode over to the local Butte Cemetery to pay my respects to the birthplace and final resting place of one of the most famous Harley-Davidson Motorcycle Daredevils to ever live, Evel Knievel. By design, I chose a route that would every five days make a stop where Evel Knievel's iconic image emanates.

After having my personal chat with Eval while standing at his gravesite, I then made haste to my first motel stop of this five-day journey. Once I'd checked in, I then walked across the street and ordered a pizza. Once back in my motel room, I showered a +1,000-mile day of dirt and road grime from my tired body and finally rolled into bed. My final thoughts before slumber hit me was that first day wasn't so bad.

Pre-Ride Day 2: 3:15 a.m., Tuesday, May 2, 2023. Outside temperature is a frigid 32 degrees Fahrenheit at mountain elevation. It is once again, and for a second day in a row, cold and dark outside. Not most bikers' idea of ideal riding conditions to say the least, but hey, my mind thought let's crank off another +1,000 miles again today just to say we can!

My vivid memories of my day two was as I headed east out of Butte, Montana, I witnessed the most beautiful Rocky

Mountain sunrise that was beyond stunning. By nightfall, and +1,000 miles later as I approached Watertown, South Dakota, off to the west the light of day closed out with one of the most striking South Dakota prairie sunsets imaginable. I stopped the motorcycle along the shoulder briefly to take in such overwhelming beauty and said my thanks for being able to experience such magnificence beyond description.

On this day, my route took me from Butte, Montana, down into the state of Wyoming then tracked east through Sturgis, Rapid City, and Sioux Falls, South Dakota, and ultimately concluded another very long day by arriving in Watertown, South Dakota, for the night. Ironically, during August of 2025, our No Boundaries Tour Ride will pass directly through the 85th Annual Sturgis Motorcycle Rally every five days. Many have questioned making my way through such a massive traffic-slowing motorcycle rally that will draw nearly 1 million bikers from across the globe, but it only seems appropriate that a world record motorcycle ride should pass through and connect with hundreds of thousands of fellow bikers also celebrating their own passion and love for motorcycle riding.

Pre-Ride Day 3: 3:00 a.m., Wednesday, May 3, 2023. Outside temperature started out at 30 degrees and ended up at 90 degrees Fahrenheit as I once again hit the high plains dessert area. Whew, a 60 degree temperature swing in one day is a test on the body. Going into this third day, I'm starting to adjust my body clock to the early morning dark departures. I must admit this morning my body feels more exhausted than the previous days. Perhaps I should have done the correct protocol of getting some hard miles in before starting my pre-ride marathon.

As this day progressed, I retraced a portion of my first day route traveling in South Dakota, North Dakota, and ending for the day in Montana. It became more difficult to maintain focus and to keep going. It felt as though my body was launching a rebellion. It is so important to maintain a good, healthy diet while maintaining one's fluid hydration when traveling out in the wind on an open motorcycle for up to 18 hours per day. The physicality of continuous wind robbing one's body of life-affirming fluids can be a cause for concern for long-distance motorcycle riders. Dehydration leads to headaches, sleepiness, and reduced reflexes. It is simply dangerous, and once a person falls into a dehydrated state, it is not quickly abated. From experience, I know it can be a real challenge to ingest enough fluids and to eat the proper nutritional specifications while logging miles upon miles for hours and hours in a day riding on a motorcycle. There is a reason many motorcycle riders agree that pushing their limits of riding a motorcycle more than a few hundred miles is a riskier choice and more discomfort than they prefer to experience.

On this day, I realized that physically and perhaps mentally, I was sitting on the threshold of struggling to maintain my pre-ride on only day three. I had a trick I utilized to take my mind off my internal troubles and force my mind to digest something other than self-pity. By this day three, my overall boredom of a third nearly 18-hour day sitting on the saddle seat of my "iron-horse" motorcycle, I came up with a way to at least make the time go faster.

I'm sure this trivia fact will do little benefit whatsoever to most road warriors, but I was able to meticulously count white hash-mark lines that are painted on all interstate highways nationwide. Did you know that there are 135 white hash mark lines for every mile of roadway? Did you also know that for every +5,000-mile rotation of my extensive world record motorcycle ride, I will continually tally over 700,000 white hash mark lines during every five-day cycle? Now here is where the ultimate adrenaline and excitement begins coursing through my body when I came to realize that upon completion of the No Boundaries Tour World Record Motorcycle Ride, my eyes will have viewed more than 1.6 million white hash marks. Let it be said, that is "white line fever" taken to the maximum, just like what the world record ride will accomplish!

Pre-Ride Day 4: 3:30 a.m., Thursday, May 4, 2023. Outside temperature is 35 degrees Fahrenheit. Today the travels took me from Belgrade, Montana, down through Buffalo, Wyoming, toward Cheyenne, Wyoming, and then toward the Colorado border, which then turned east onto Interstate I-80 riding nearly all the way across the flatlands of Nebraska, and finally ending up for the night in Lincoln, Nebraska. Thankfully today, my route took me far enough on a southerly route that the temperatures finally stabilized around the 60 degrees range for much of the day, which felt like paradise after traveling the first portion of the trip with half-day frigid temperatures. I'd failed to mention that during the earlier pre-trip days, when starting the first portion of the day each morning, with the temperatures at or below freezing, along with facing a headwind while riding a motorcycle at 80 mph, I can most definitely assure you there is a minus sub-zero windchill that brings a magnitude of internal and external chills. It often felt like warmth would never come as those endless miles kept tallying up.

I'm unsure if the more seasonal and warmer weather helped irrevocably boost my spirits, giving me what felt like a newfound second wind, or perhaps it was simply the element that after four grueling days at over +1,000 miles per day, I'd at last acclimated to the rigors of my motorcycling pre-ride.

As I lie in bed on my fourth night, excitement stirs within me to finish my five-day pre-ride when the morrow comes. I even found it difficult to fall asleep on this my fourth night even after logging an astounding 4,155 miles in a mere four days of motorcycling. Bring on tomorrow!

Pre-Ride Day 5: 3:05 a.m., Friday, May 5, 2023. Outside temperature is 48 degrees Fahrenheit. Today the travels took me from Lincoln and on to Omaha, Nebraska, then traveling through

NO BOUNDARIES TOUR

Sioux City, Iowa, and then a long "deadhead" motorcycle ride up through eastern South Dakota, as well as all the way up through eastern North Dakota to Pembina, North Dakota. This is located right on the Canadian International Border Crossing. From the Canadian line, I went on to retrace my route back south to Casselton, North Dakota, turned back southwesterly and traveled Interstate I-94 back from North Dakota until reaching my home base near St. Cloud, Minnesota.

Just imagine covering a grand total of 5,184 miles in under five days while logging over 85 hours sitting on the seat of a motorcycle. Try to put that into perspective for those who work a 40-hour work week for their career. Now try to imagine putting in 85 hours every five days and repeatedly again every five days for a total of 120 days consecutively. That time card would equate to over 2,040 hours of motorcycle riding time in just four months. That is almost equal to an entire 52 weeks of working an average of 40 hours per week and would equate to 2,080 hours for working an entire year of your career.

Is there anyone who doesn't feel this No Boundaries Tour Ride is a rather serious commitment and endeavor?

Okay, we knocked off the five-day, 5,184-mile pre-ride practice trip.

After submitting all the travel logs, the maps, all the documentation, and the fuel receipts to the Iron Butt Association, this ride was officially certified as an official IBA Saddle Sore 5,000 completed within five twenty-four-hour days of riding.

One might envision that with this dedicated +5,000-mile pre-ride practice trip over, would it be fair to conclude that I'd be able to rest for a spell? Oh, but think again, my friends. As the time clock keeps winding down toward that inevitable start deadline of May 2025 for the official start of the No Boundaries Tour Ride, my next task was to immediately travel the over 6,500 miles while retracing my entire motorcycle's route using my automobile to then travel out and meet face-to-face with each and every one of the seventeen tremendously dedicated Harley-Davidson Dealerships positioned all along the seven state semicircular route that I'll be traveling past over and over again on my ride in 2025.

The reasoning for these mandatory HD dealership meetings was because it was essential to meet with all their key dealership owners, management, and key personnel to spell out some very important needs prior to and during the No Boundaries Tour World Record Motorcycle Charity Ride.

Here is a partial wish list that might be offered by any and/or all the Harley-Davidson dealerships along the 2025 NBT Ride route.

1. Service work and oil changes every 5–10 days (5,000–10,000 miles).
2. Full front and rear tire replacement every 10 days (10,000 miles).
3. Emergency service repair and motorcycle pickup in an emergency.
4. Dealership customer appreciation events with fundraising options.
5. Help organize "customer meet and greet" sessions.
6. Facilitate biker "ride-along" dates as a fundraiser.
7. Dedicated product sales toward "fight human trafficking."
8. Assistance to comp a motel room in their town.
9. Comp assistance for some meal expenses.
10. Comp assistance for some fuel expenses.
11. Comp assistance for HD dealership mechanical, parts, and service work.

The following contains the notes obtained during the September 5, 6, 7, 8 and October 24 and 25, 2023, NBT Ride HD dealer visits/notes.

NO BOUNDARIES TOUR

NBT Ride HD Dealer Visits/Notes

Face-to-Face Visits: September 5, 6, 7, 8 and October 24, 25, 2023
(Logged 6,500 total miles)

1. **Viking Land HD GM: Dan, Debbie (Wife) Glucky**

   3555 Shadowwood Dr. NE 320-251-6980 (Wk)
   St. Cloud, MN. 56379 320-774-1140 (Cell)
   dglucky@vikinglandHD.com

   They are very receptive to working with us on the NBT Ride. They are a major NBT Ride sponsor as I purchased new 2023 HD Road Glide being displayed on their showroom floor. They have agreed to sell all required parts for 15% over dealer cost. Major service work to be done on bike here. I have a four-year unlimited milage HD warranty on this bike.

2. **Apol's HD GM: Tom Brenden**

   1515 42nd Ave. W. 320-763-9800
   Alexandria, MN. 56308
   tom.brenden@apols.com

   I talked with GM Tom Brenden, and he passed along all the NBT Ride information to Apol's HD dealership owners, Robin and Lannie Apol. They also have a HD dealership in Raymond, MN, which I also made a face-to-face visit to discuss NBT Ride information on Oct. 25, 2023.

3. **HD of Fargo Owners: Jimmy and Joe Entenman (Away)**

   701 Christianson Dr. GM: Adrian Smith (Away)
   West Fargo, ND. 58078 Sales/Merchandizing Mgr.: Katie
   701-277-1000

Dealership is partnered with J & L HD of Sioux Falls, SD, and Glacial Lakes HD of Watertown, SD. I spoke with Sales/Merchandizing Mgr. Katie, and she was going to pass along all the NBT Ride Information along to the Management team.

4.　Stutsman HD GM: John Seifert

2501 3rd Ave SW Owner: Karl Christian (Away)
Jamestown, NS. 58401701-252-5271 (Wk)
701-261-9283 (Cell)
johnseifert@stutsmanhd.com

They are very receptive to working with us on the NBT Ride.

5.　Rough Rider HD Owner: Bill and Carol (wife) Stork

3708 Memorial Hwy.701-663-2220 (Wk)
Mandan, ND. 58554GM: DJ Wallace

We talked with the owner, Bill (Coyote: Nickname) and GM DJ Wallace. They are very receptive to working with us on the NBT Ride.

6.　Copper Canyon HD GMs: Whitney and Curtis Moen

34 Olympic Way (Ultra-Marathons)
Butte, MT. 59701406-782-5601 (Wk)
406-788-1268 (Cell)
w.moenharley@gmail.com

I talked with Whitney, and her parents own this Butte, MT, HD dealership as well as Great Falls, MT. Whitney and her husband Curtis have managed this HD dealership since 2010. She was very excited about supporting our NBT Ride.

NO BOUNDARIES TOUR

7. **Yellowstone HD Owner/GM: Josh Fry**

I met with their entire dealership team, and they were very receptive to supporting our NBT Ride.

8. **Beartooth HD Marketing Mgr.: Ann Marie Usher**

6900 S. Frontage Rd. Owner: Barry Usher (Away) Billings, MT 59101 406-252-2888 (WK) 406-671-9001 (Cell) CFO: Kersti Maharrey (Away) annmarie@beartoothharley.com Bus. Mgr.: Richard Marciel (Away)

I met with Marketing Manager Ann Marie Usher, and she was very receptive to having their dealership working with the NBT Ride. We talked about an evening gathering, fund-raiser, etc.

9. **Deluxe HD Owner: Maria Raque**

3300 Conestoga Dr. GM: Mike Raque Gillette, WY. 82718 307-687-2001 (Wk) (2nd Dealership in Sundance, WY) maria@chuckdeluxe.com mike@chuckdeluxe.com

I talked with both Maria and Mike Raque, and they showed interest in supporting the NBT Ride.

10. **Black Hills HD Marketing Mgr.: Mike Maloney**

2820 Harley Dr. 605-342-9362 (Wk) Rapid City, SD. 57702 605-209-5009 (Cell) mike@blackhillshd.com GM: Kelly Rang

I've stopped and met with this dealership twice due to the huge Sturgis Motorcycle Rally connection. Mike Maloney will be our main NBT Ride contact to develop support from this Dealership.

11. J & L HD Owners: Jim and Joe Entamen (Away)

2601 W 60th St. N.GM: Nate Wentzel (Met on 9/7/23)
Sioux Falls, SD. 57107605-334-2721 (Wk)
Nate.wentzel@jlharleydavidson.com
Marketing Mgr.: May Rodriguez
(Met on 3/23/23)

They have multidealerships with Glacial Lakes HD of Watertown, SD, and HD of Fargo of West Fargo, ND. I've met with this dealership twice, first with May, the marketing manager, and then on another visit with GM Nate Wentzel. They are showing interest in supporting our NBT Ride.

12. High Country HD GM: Christy McAffee

3320 E. Lincolnway 307-432-2195 (Direct line)
Cheyenne, WY. 82001307-638-8307 (Wk)
Christy.mcaffee@highcountryharley.com

I met with Christy, and she will talk with their other Frederick, CO, dealership and the owners about supporting the NBT Ride.

13. Frontier HD Creative Director: Chloe Ekberg

205 NW 40th St.402-616-0536
Lincoln, NE. 68528 (chloee@frontierhd.com)
Marketing Director: Hollie Pille
VP Operations: Chad (Away)
402-466-9100 (Wk)

GM: Rich (Met him)
holliep@frontierhd.com

I met with both Chloe and Hollie, and they want to play a big role in doing supportive activities for the NBT Ride. Evening fundraisers, ride-alongs, etc.

14. Defiance HD GM: Nick Doerr

4940 S. 72nd St. 402-331-0022 (Wk)
Omaha, NE. 68127
nickd@defiancehd.com

I met with Nick, and he will pass along all the NBT Ride information to his dealership teams.

15. Dillon Brothers HD GM: Tom Kindler

3838 N. Cleveland Blvd. 402-505-4252 (Direct)
Omaha, NE. 68116 402-289-5556 (Wk)
Owners: Blake and Sid Dillion
sales@dillonharley.com

Met with GM Tom Kindler and he will pass along the NBT Ride Information to the Owners who were away during my visit. Dillon Brothers has a second HD Dealership at 2440 E. 23rd St., Freemont, NE.

16. Roosters HD GM: Robert Trupe (Away)

1930 N Lewis Blvd. Exec. Asst.: Jamie Hoffman
Sioux City, IA. 51105 712-252-2750 (Wk)
Jamie.h@roostersh-d.com
General Merchandising Mgr.: Tonya Monk
tonya@roostersh-d.com

I had a lengthy meeting with both Jamie Hoffman and Tonya Monk. They are very excited to have their dealership support and hold some events with NBT Ride.

17. Glacial Lakes HD 605-886-3448

1000 19th St. SE Store Mgr.: Tommy Myers
Watertown, SD. 57201
tommy@jlharleydavidson.com
Motor Clothes Sales: Kalie Overgaard
(Boyfriend is Nate Wentzel J&L Sales Mgr.)
glmc@jlharleydavidson.com

They are very excited to do activities. (They will try to comp the hotel.) They will do a "Make a Wish" ride and event on June 14 and 15, 2024.

CHAPTER 11

Ride of a Lifetime Specifics

Way back in chapter one of this book, I raised the question whenever there was a remarkable outcome to a challenging circumstance, "Was that something of just sheer luck, or was it possibly a miracle, but perhaps it was only a simple coincidence?" Again, in my heart, I don't feel there are really any coincidences with God but rather I believe that God orchestrates each and everything within His very specific plan for us His children of God.

As I write this portion of the story, it's now less than one year away from the start of my biggest lifetime goal. As someone who is at the brink of 70 years, I'd be remiss to not admit I'm often questioning the sanity of making such a marathon attempt at logging so many miles on a motorcycle. The idea alone is enough to break the will and spirit of others one-half or even one-third the age of seventy. Have I had a few second thoughts as each passing month gets closer to the start date? YES!

Ironically, and in my heart, I felt it no coincidence again, as I stumbled upon watching a biographical sports drama film that left me reinvigorated to reach my goal. My courage to pursue and conquer this dream became evermore real, as my demeanor changed after watching the movie *Nyad*. The movie features actress Annette Bening as a long-distance marathon swimmer, along with actress Jodie Foster as her persistent swimming coach. This movie showed the remarkable true story of athlete Diana Nyad who, at the age of sixty and with the help of her best friend and coach, commits to achieving her lifelong dream: a 110-mile open ocean swim from Cuba to Florida.

A riveting tale of the life of world-class athlete Diana Nyad. Three decades after giving up marathon swimming in exchange for a prominent career as a sports journalist, at the age of sixty, Diana becomes obsessed with completing an epic swim that always eluded her. The 110-mile trek from Cuba to Florida is often referred to as the "Mount Everest" of swims. Determined to become the first person to finish the swim without a shark cage, Diana goes on a thrilling four-year journey with her best friend and coach Bonnie Stoll and a dedicated sailing team.

Diana Nyad made her first unsuccessful attempt at the age of sixty-one. She tried and failed repeatedly as the ocean currents and stinging and dangerous sea creatures held her back, and yet she obtained her remarkable outcome to a challenging circumstance, "Was that something of just sheer luck, or was it possibly a miracle? Perhaps it was only a simple coincidence," but again, in my heart, I don't feel there are really any coincidences with God. I rather believe that God orchestrates each and everything within His very specific plan for us His children of God.

So we are under one year away with the preparations and tasks gaining momentum for the No Boundaries Tour World Record Charity Ride departing on May 25, 2025.

CHAPTER 12

Campaign Against Human Trafficking

The clock continues to tick down with an ever-decreasing time to mentally, physically, financially, and organizationally prepare. We **MUST PULL OFF** the "Mount Everest" of all marathons with one of the most notable long-distance endurance motorcycle charity rides ever attempted!

****

The No Boundaries Tour Ride team has continuously worked overtime to coordinate such a massive undertaking. It has and it will continue to require an entire village of teamwork for the ultimate success story to reach completion. The team, the friends, the family, the colleagues, the sponsors, the donors, and the countless supporters have provided their cumulative labors of love, support, prayers, donated time, phone calls, ride-alongs, media interviews, route media scheduling, group interaction scheduling, motorcycle servicing planning, meal planning, physical training specifics, and health monitoring to name a very short action list. There are literally thousands of details to be managed for this endeavor's success.

PASSING ALONG MY HEARTFELD THANK YOU WILL NEVER BE NEARLY ENOUGH TO EXPRESS MY DEEPEST

SCOTT D. GOTTSCHALK

GRATITUDE FOR ALL OF YOUR EFFORTS AND FOR ALL OF YOUR SELFLESS ROLES THAT YOU PERFORMED TO MAKE THIS A TRUE SUCCESS STORY!!!

OUR CAMPAIGN HAS INVIGORATED A NEWFOUND MOVEMENT TO STOP HUMAN TRAFFICKING. KEEP PUSHING YOUR BOUNDARIES AND CONTINUE THE FIGHT.

No Boundaries Tour Ride Action Plans and Upcoming Work Assignments

- Monthly NBT Ride team Zoom conference meeting sessions.
- Quarterly NBT Ride team "in-person" meeting assemblies.
- September 2024 - Participate in an international Motivational Missions "Stop Human Trafficking" youth training events at schools within the country of Jamaica.
- Continuous sponsorship and donor contacts requesting financial contributions and/or contributions "in-kind."

    1. Motel/hotel comps (120 nights)
    2. Petroleum company comps ($20,000 for motorcycle fuel)
    3. Airline company comps (Reduction in nationwide air travel)
    4. Motorcycle tire company comps (24 motorcycle tires)
    5. Food, meal, restaurant comps (meal intake, 120 days on the road)
    6. Clothing and equipment comps (riding and motorcycle gear)
    7. Local fundraising (gatherings, open house events, live music)

8. Marketing materials comps (brochures, patches, caps, T-shirts)
9. Coordinate speaking engagements (meetings and events)
10. Motorcycle servicing comps (5-day service, 10-day new tires)
11. Support vehicle comps (vehicle, fuel, miscellaneous expenses)
12. Electronics, video, and camera comps (complete documentation)
13. Medical health monitoring and nutritionist dietary support
14. Physical training coach/mentor

- Constant media releases, NBT Ride updates, scheduling interviews for magazines, newspapers, radio, television, and social media awareness campaigns.

Collaborative Journey to Combat Human Trafficking

As a continuation of the unfolding No Boundaries Ride Tour chronicle unfolds, we were amazingly guided toward forming a valued partnership with Victor Williams, founder/CEO of Quest2Freedom, Inc. Victor is a (retired) special agent with Homeland Security Investigations. Quest2Freedom is on a mission driven by the core values encapsulated in their mission statement: **"To end human trafficking and exploitation globally."** Their relentless pursuit of justice is underpinned by a steadfast commitment to raising awareness, supporting survivors, and advocating for systemic and cultural changes that foster a world where dignity, respect, and freedom reign supreme.

The narrative delves into the collaborative efforts between Quest2Freedom and a multitude of community partners, law enforcement agencies, governments, and nongovernmental organizations. Through a united front, they strive to safeguard communities, hold traffickers accountable, and deliver justice to survivors of human trafficking. With a shared vision and unwavering resolve, they forge alliances that transcend boundaries and confront the malevolent forces that seek to profit from human trafficking.

Quest2Freedom emerges as a beacon of hope in the fight against human trafficking armed with a relentless dedication to dismantling the criminal infrastructure perpetuating this abominable crime. There is a call to action, emphasizing the importance of addressing human trafficking from a holistic cultural perspective. By unraveling the cultural roots that nourish the insidious tendrils of human trafficking, Quest2Freedom sheds light on the critical avenues of prevention, protection, prosecution, and partnership that are indispensable in eradicating this pervasive global issue.

Victor Williams, a stalwart advocate in the realm of human trafficking, brings forth over three decades of domestic and international law enforcement experience to the forefront of this transformative endeavor. His visionary leadership catalyzes a movement toward cultural awareness and education as pivotal tools in combatting human trafficking. Through Quest2Freedom, he embarks on a journey to educate and empower individuals, fostering partnerships, conducting workshops, and igniting a collective consciousness aimed at effecting real change in the fight against human trafficking.

Within the narrative, Victor's impactful initiatives unfold, from his tenure as a security consultant for the Atlanta Basketball Club to his role as the coordinator of The Georgia Coalition to Combat Human Trafficking. His tireless efforts garner accolades and recognition, underscoring his unwavering dedication to the cause. As a respected instructor, presenter, and coordinator, Victor galvanizes international law enforcement officers worldwide, imparting essential knowledge on prevention, victim protection, offender prosecution, and collaborative partnerships in the fight against human trafficking.

Awards and honors punctuate Victor's illustrious career, serving as testaments to his unwavering commitment to justice and compassion in the face of human suffering. From Congressional accolades to esteemed recognition in the law enforcement realm, Victor's impact reverberates far and wide, illuminating a path toward empathy, solidarity, and transformative action in combating human trafficking.

The journey depicted within these pages underscores the multifaceted approach adopted by Quest2Freedom in assisting victims of human trafficking. Through emergency response measures and immediate support in the form of short-term hotel stays and transportation services, the organization extends a lifeline to those trapped in the harrowing throes of exploitation.

To further amplify the clarion call against human trafficking, Quest2Freedom leverages speaking engagements, podcast series, and comprehensive training and awareness programs. These platforms serve as conduits for spreading critical knowledge, empowering communities, and fostering a collective resilience against the scourge of human trafficking.

The concluding chapter spotlights a poignant podcast featuring Victor Williams, Scott Gottschalk of NBT Ride, and Alexa Oliva from Motivational Missions. This collective effort encapsulates the spirit of unity, collaboration, and unwavering determination that defines the No Boundaries Tour World Record Motorcycle Charity Ride. Their impassioned dialogue underscores the urgent need to combat human trafficking and galvanize a global movement toward freedom, justice, and human dignity.

The No Boundaries Tour stands as a testament to the transformative power of unity, advocacy, and unwavering resolve in the fight against human trafficking. Through the collaborative efforts of visionaries like Victor Williams and dedicated partners across the globe, the narrative echoes a resounding call to action: **"Let us stand united, let us raise our voices, and let us forge a world where no boundaries impede the pursuit of justice for all."**

****

Thank you, Victor, for your selfless efforts to fight this horrible global human trafficking crime wave. I firmly believe that God aligned the stars for our paths to converge, and I commit to do everything within our power to spread the word and make a monumental impact to get this travesty of human trafficking stopped!!!

NBT Ride Launch Reception
4:00–8:00 p.m., Saturday, May 24, 2025

Peterson Harley-Davidson in Miami, Florida

Excitement has been building for months since the confirmation of two outstanding performers who have commitment to perform during the May 24, 2024, NBT Ride launch reception.

Our first VIP performer will be Crystal Sierra Rodgers, known as the "Queen of Latin Hip-Hop," is a powerful singer, songwriter, actress, and music producer. Crystal Sierra, aka Crystal Rodgers, graduated from Baltimore School for the Arts where she was classically trained to sing opera music. It was there that she became friends with Tupac Shakur. Wanting to study more genres and absorb all that entertainment had to offer, Crystal obtained a scholarship from Berklee College of Music where she performed with salsa and Latin jazz bands influenced by her Colombian roots.

She left Berklee to move to Los Angeles and began to simultaneously pursue her singing and acting career, studying under the direction of many great coaches to include Ivana Chubbuck's Studio. While recording one night in the studio, she met and was later managed by casting director Robbi Reed who suggested that she audition for the role of "Angel" (Tupac Shakur's baby mama) in John Singleton's movie *Poetic Justice*.

Shortly thereafter, Crystal Sierra signed her first record deal with The Aftermath in which she joined a female group called Hands-On and co-wrote "Got Me Open" on Dr. Dre's label. The compilation release was a success and went platinum! "The Queen of Latin Hip-Hop" had an opportunity to be the Latin solo artist she always dreamed of and signed her second major record deal with Virgin Records where she released her single "Playa No Mor" off her *Morena* album while still acting in various television shows and stage plays. She recently earned her associate degree graduating with cum laude honors from the Los Angeles Film School in Hollywood, CA. With more fervor, determination, and focus, this superstar is returning to the stage, working on her newest album and upcoming film projects.

Crystal is very passionate about helping make a statement to stop human trafficking during her performance at the NBT Ride launch reception. She may even write and perform a special human trafficking theme song with a potent message for her audience to witness.

Thank you, Crystal, for being such a major gift for our endeavor to stop human trafficking.

Our second VIP performer will be DJ Epps, Omar Epps who is an American actor, rapper, and producer. He has been awarded nine NAACP Image Awards, two Teen Choice Awards, one MTV Movie Award, one Black Reel Award, and one Screen Actors Guild Award. Epps's film roles include *Juice, Higher Learning, The Wood, In Too Deep,* and *Love & Basketball.* His television work includes the role of Dr. Dennis Gant on the medical drama series *ER*, J. Martin Bellamy in *Resurrection*, Dr. Eric Foreman on the Fox medical drama series *House* from 2004–2012, and Isaac Johnson in the TV series *Shooter* from 2016–2018.

Thank you so much, DJ, for your part at the NBT Ride launch reception. You are a true blessing, and please accept our most sincere appreciation for your efforts toward stopping human trafficking.

TOGETHER, WE WILL ALL MAKE AN IMPACT!

CHAPTER 14

Mission Accomplished

The No Boundaries Tour Charity Ride may be over, but the adventure continues! Starting December 1st, 2025, you can get your hands on the final chapter with all the details, results, and highlights. Download it instantly from Amazon.com or order a printed copy to keep as a souvenir.

CHAPTER 14

Motorcycling Quotes, Memes, and Laughter

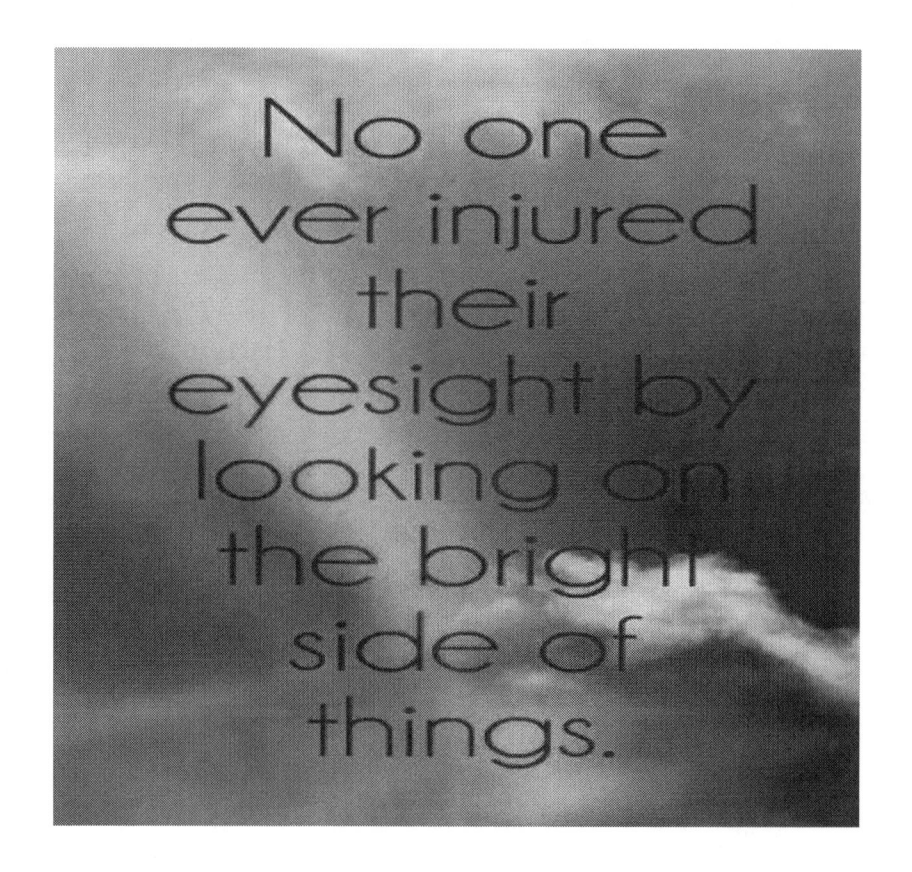

No one ever injured their eyesight by looking on the bright side of things.

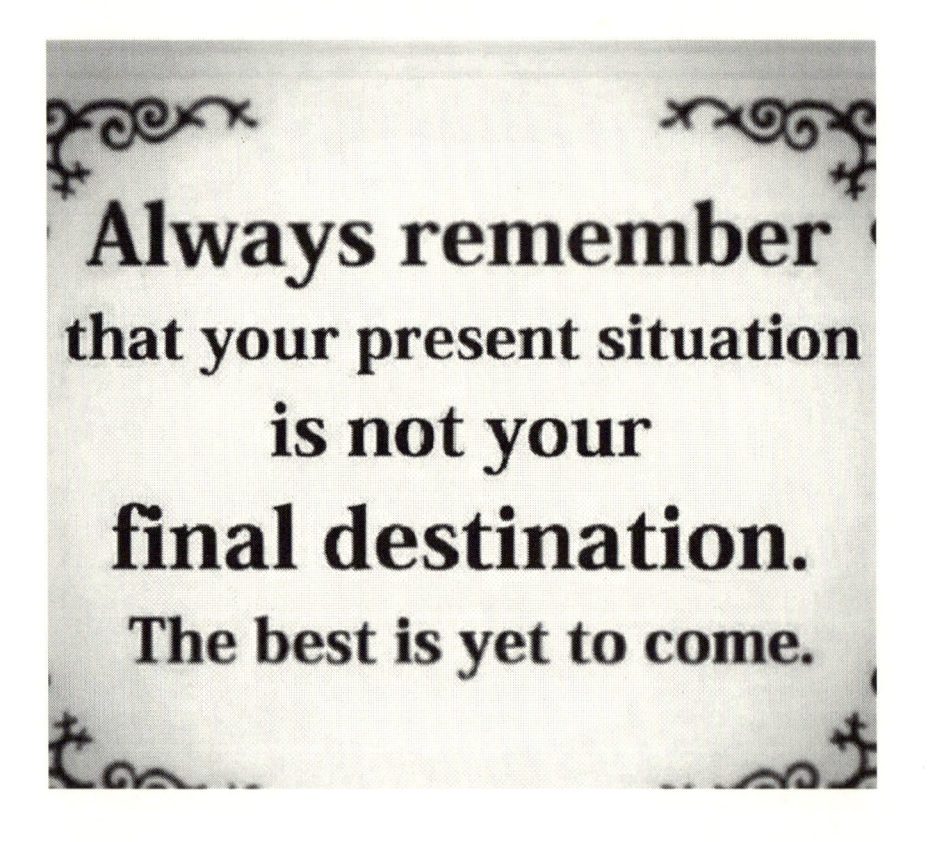

> **Always remember** that your present situation is not your final destination. The best is yet to come.

NO BOUNDARIES TOUR

Don't die before you're dead.

SCOTT D. GOTTSCHALK

> YOU CAN NOT LIVE A POSITIVE LIFE, WITH A NEGATIVE MIND.

@BERTOLIVA
WWW.BERTOLIVA.COM

BERT OLIVA
LEADERSHIP & HUMAN BEHAVIOR EXPERT

NO BOUNDARIES TOUR

SCOTT D. GOTTSCHALK

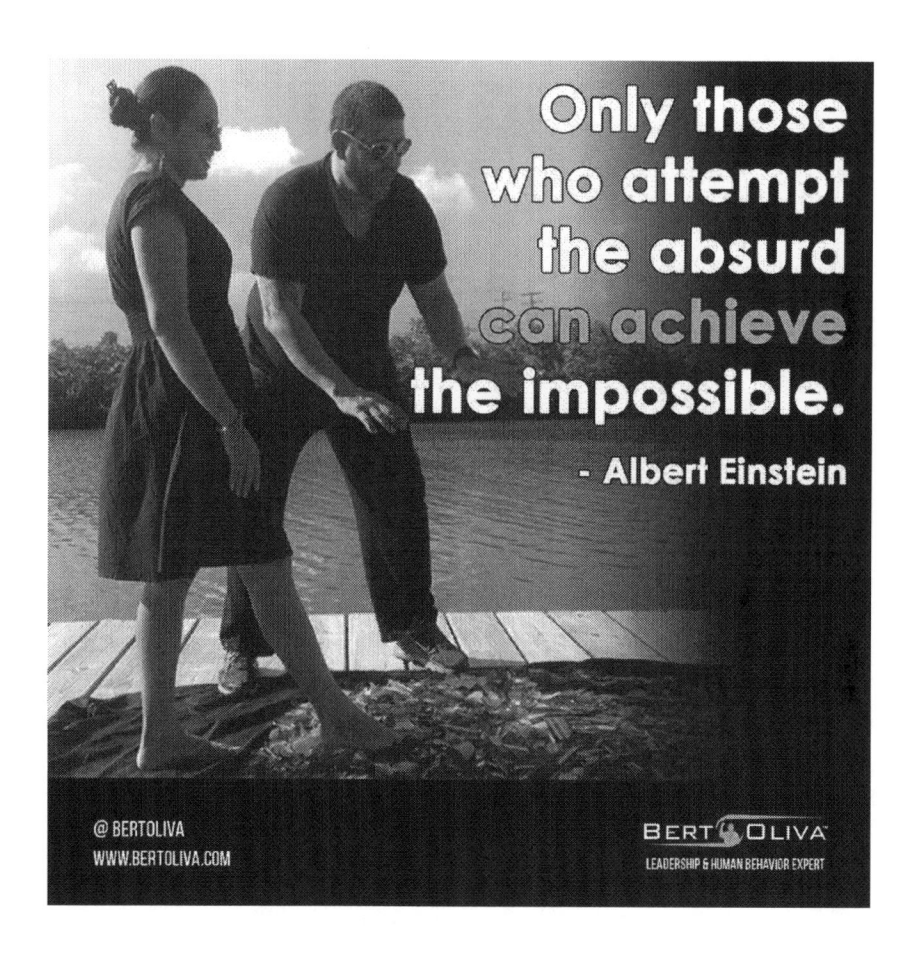

NO BOUNDARIES TOUR

> Only those who attempt the absurd can achieve the impossible.
>
> - Albert Einstein

@ BERTOLIVA
WWW.BERTOLIVA.COM

BERT OLIVA
LEADERSHIP & HUMAN BEHAVIOR EXPERT

SCOTT D. GOTTSCHALK

WHEN YOU'RE TOO OLD TO RIDE YOUR HARLEY

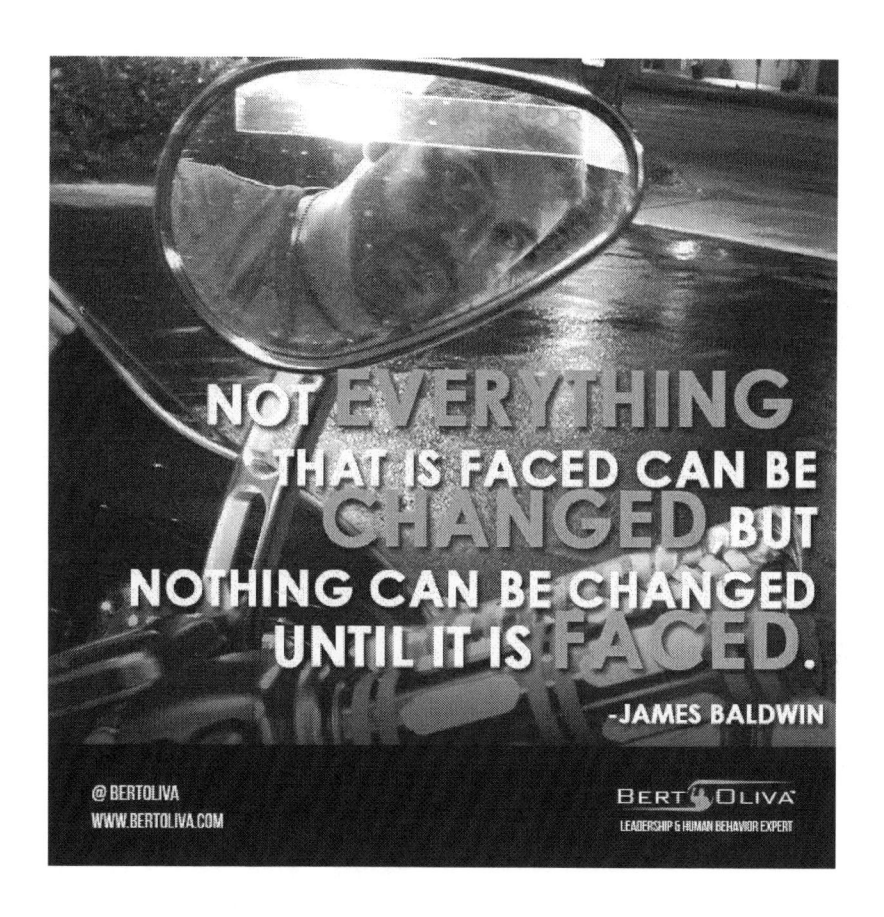

NO BOUNDARIES TOUR

> NOT EVERYTHING THAT IS FACED CAN BE CHANGED, BUT NOTHING CAN BE CHANGED UNTIL IT IS FACED.
>
> —JAMES BALDWIN

@BERTOLIVA
WWW.BERTOLIVA.COM

BERT OLIVA
LEADERSHIP & HUMAN BEHAVIOR EXPERT

"DON'T WAIT FOR THE PERFECT MOMENT. TAKE THE MOMENT AND MAKE IT PERFECT."

-ZOEY SAYWARD

@BERTOLIVA
WWW.BERTOLIVA.COM

BERT OLIVA
LEADERSHIP & HUMAN BEHAVIOR EXPERT

> WHEN YOU CATCH A GLIMPSE OF YOUR POTENTIAL, THAT'S WHEN PASSION IS BORN.
> —ZIG ZIGLAR

SCOTT D. GOTTSCHALK

> DO NOT GO WHERE THE PATH MAY LEAD, GO INSTEAD WHERE THERE IS NO PATH AND LEAVE A TRAIL

NO BOUNDARIES TOUR

We only live once, snoopy.

Wrong! we only die once.
We live every day!

SCOTT D. GOTTSCHALK

> DON'T WORRY ABOUT THOSE WHO TALK BEHIND YOUR BACK, THEY'RE BEHIND YOU FOR A REASON.

NO BOUNDARIES TOUR

Enjoy life. It has an expiration date

SCOTT D. GOTTSCHALK

Time is like a river. You cannot touch the same water twice, because the flow that has passed will never pass again. Enjoy every moment of your life.

NO BOUNDARIES TOUR

> **DO THE WORK OTHERS AREN'T WILLING TO DO AND YOU'LL GET THE THING'S OTHERS WILL NEVER HAVE**
> INSPIRATIONAL THEORY

> A PESSIMIST SEES THE DIFFICULTY IN EVERY OPPORTUNITY; AN OPTIMIST SEES THE OPPORTUNITY IN EVERY DIFFICULTY.
>
> – WINSTON CHURCHILL

> I never thought I would see a time that so many people were so afraid of dying that they were willing to stop living.

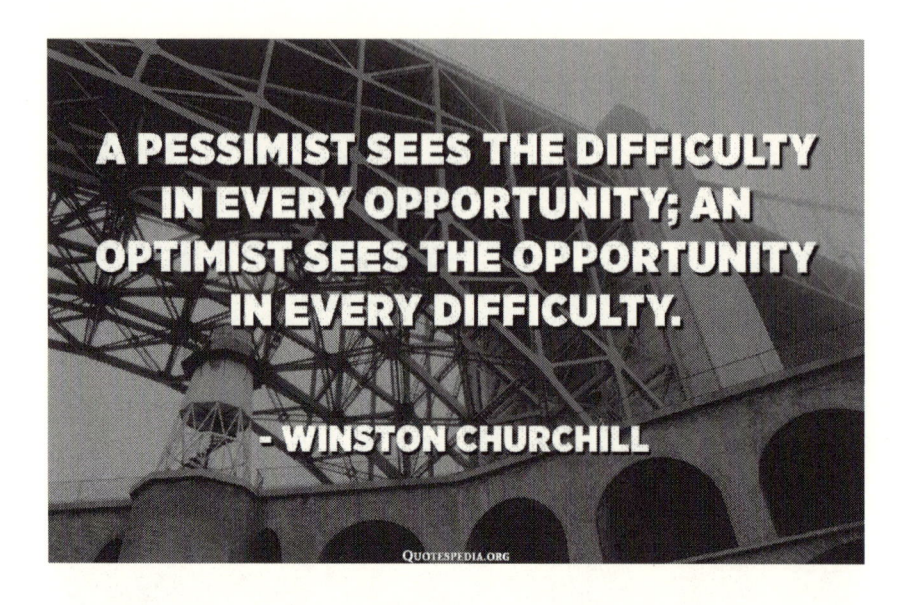

NO BOUNDARIES TOUR

SCOTT D. GOTTSCHALK

> Tell me I can't, then watch me work twice as hard to prove you wrong.

NO BOUNDARIES TOUR

> THERE'S A SPIRITUAL SIDE TO RIDING A MOTORCYCLE... IT'S A STATE OF MIND. THAT PLACE WHERE YOU LOSE YOURSELF AND FIND YOURSELF...

SCOTT D. GOTTSCHALK

THE IDEA IS TO DIE YOUNG AS LATE AS POSSIBLE

NO BOUNDARIES TOUR

> The COST of not following your heart, is spending the rest of your life WISHING you had...

If what doesn't kill you makes you stronger, I'd say by now I'm pretty indestructible.

NO BOUNDARIES TOUR

SCOTT D. GOTTSCHALK

> A HUNDRED YEARS FROM NOW MY GREAT GRAND KIDS WILL NOT RECALL MY BANK BALANCE, THE SORT OF HOUSE I LIVED IN, OR THE KIND OF CAR I DROVE... BUT THEY WILL REMEMBER I RODE A "MOTORCYCLE"

NO BOUNDARIES TOUR

SCOTT D. GOTTSCHALK

> "ATTACK LIFE, IT'S GOING TO KILL YOU ANYWAY."
> —Steve Mcqueen

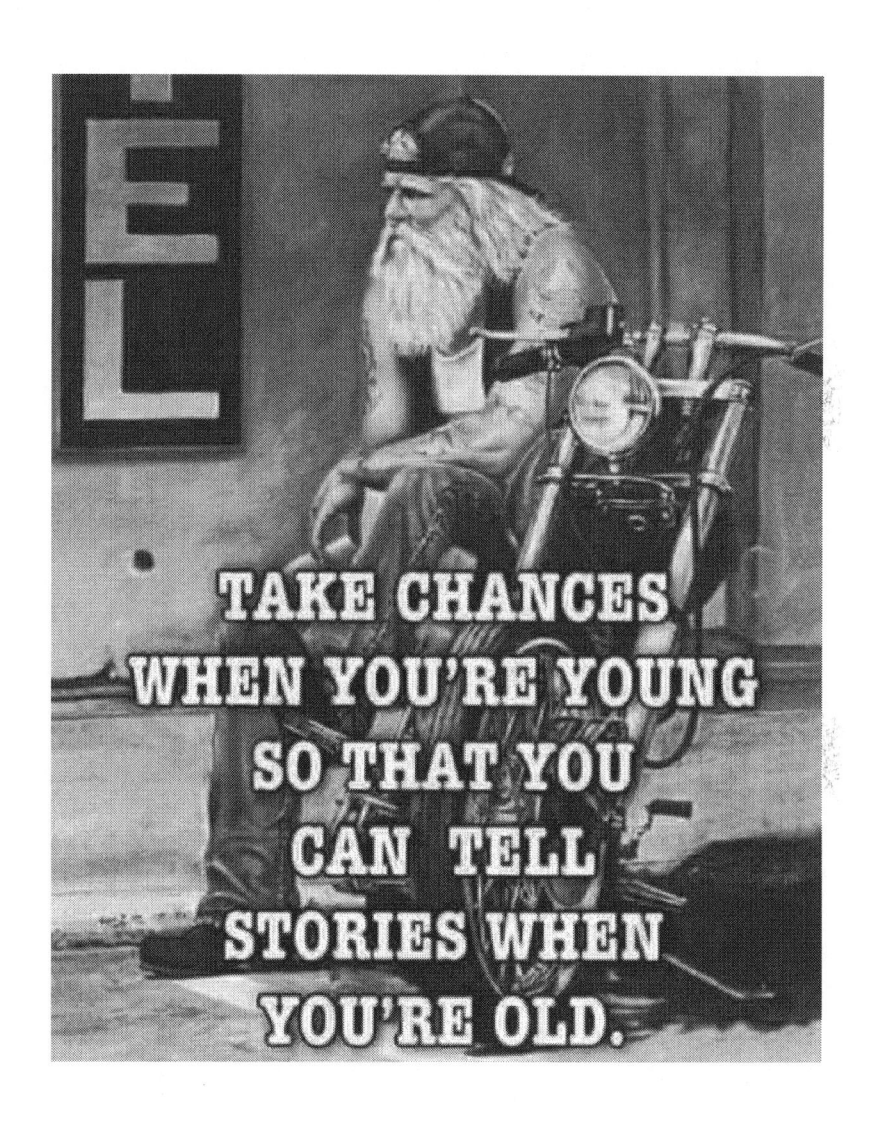

TAKE CHANCES WHEN YOU'RE YOUNG SO THAT YOU CAN TELL STORIES WHEN YOU'RE OLD.

SCOTT D. GOTTSCHALK

> There are times I really enjoy riding alone, it's just me, my problems, and the wind to wash them away.

> If I die riding my bike, don't cry for me instead smile for me and know I died doing what I love and with a smile on my face.

NO BOUNDARIES TOUR

> One day you'll just be a memory for some people. Do your best to be a good one.

THE WISE YOU

SCOTT D. GOTTSCHALK

> IT'S YOUR ROAD
> OTHERS CAN RIDE IT WITH YOU
> BUT NO ONE CAN RIDE IT FOR YOU

NO BOUNDARIES TOUR

> You're A Biker When You Ride
> A Motorcycle Not So The
> World Can See You..
> But So You Can See The World.

> I haven't been everywhere.
> But it's on my list.

SCOTT D. GOTTSCHALK

SOME OF THE BEST ADVENTURES HAVEN'T HAPPENED YET...

KEEP ON RIDING...

IT'S AMAZING THE NUMBER OF GREAT PEOPLE IN MY LIFE THAT I WOULDN'T HAVE EVER MET IF IT WASN'T FOR MOTORCYLES

SCOTT D. GOTTSCHALK

NO BOUNDARIES TOUR

May your motorcycle always take you

where your heart wants to go . . .

SCOTT D. GOTTSCHALK

The most dangerous risk of all. The risk of spending your life not doing what you want.

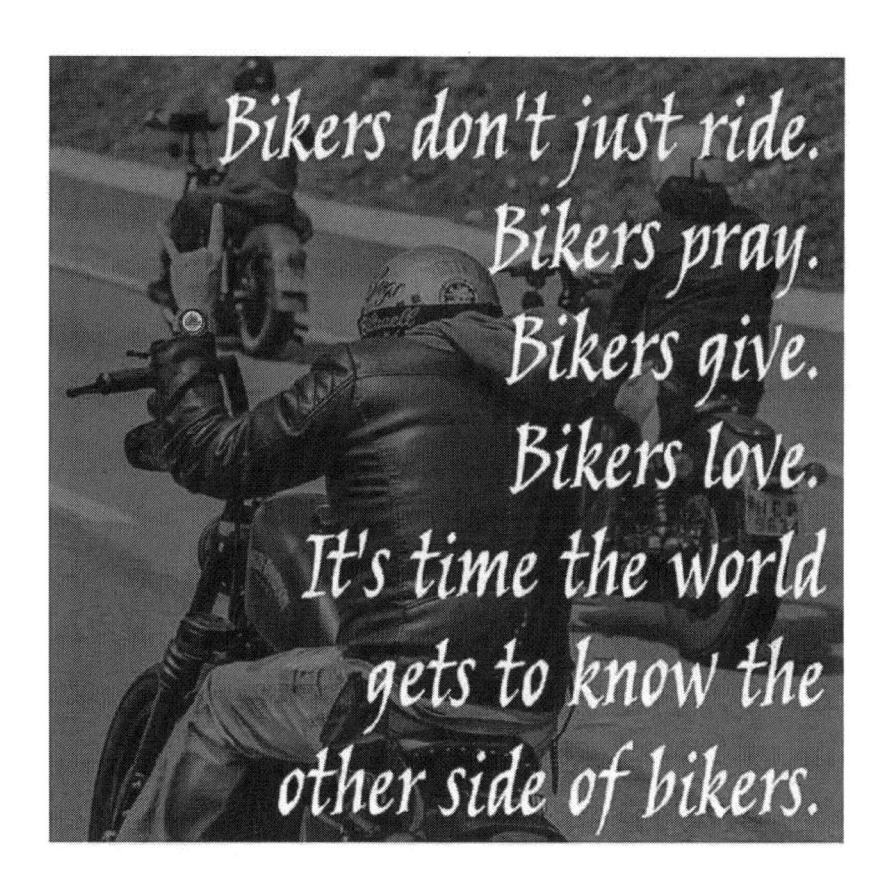

Bikers don't just ride.
Bikers pray.
Bikers give.
Bikers love.
It's time the world gets to know the other side of bikers.

SCOTT D. GOTTSCHALK

The Average Person Burns 175 To 225 Calorie An Hour While Riding On A Motorcycle

I Don't Need To Go On A Diet, I Just Need To Ride More!

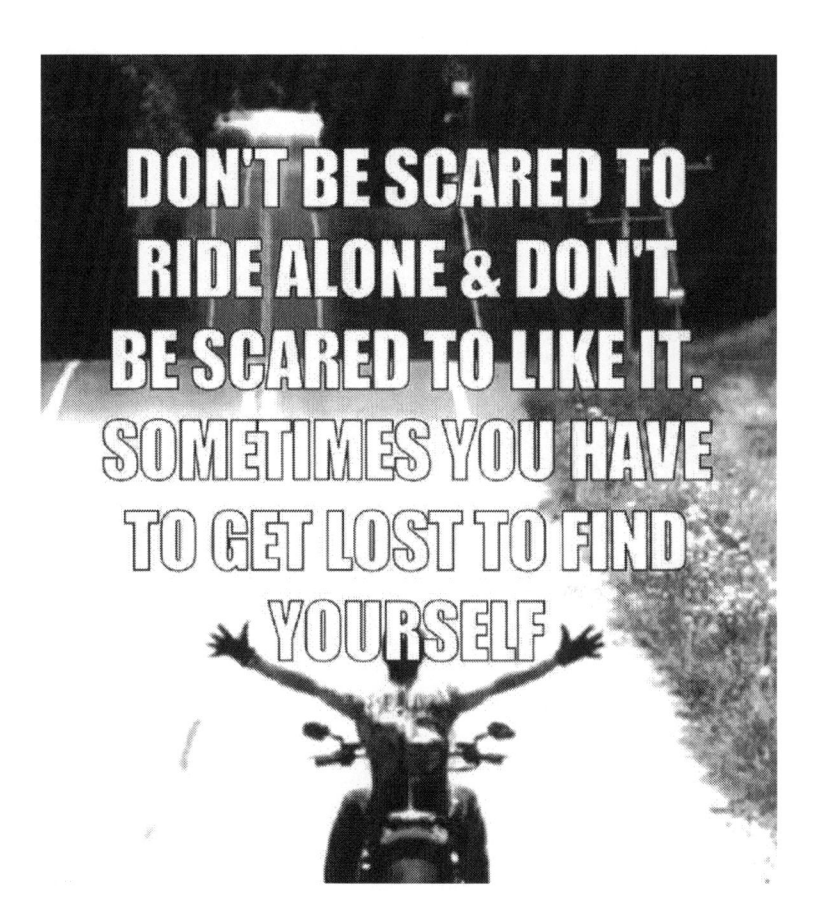

NO BOUNDARIES TOUR

> DON'T BE SCARED TO RIDE ALONE & DON'T BE SCARED TO LIKE IT. SOMETIMES YOU HAVE TO GET LOST TO FIND YOURSELF

SCOTT D. GOTTSCHALK

> I tried to be normal once.
>
> Worst two minutes of my life.
>
> – unknown

> I WANT TO INSPIRE PEOPLE. I WANT SOMEONE TO LOOK AT ME AND SAY "BECAUSE OF YOU I DIDN'T GIVE UP."

SCOTT D. GOTTSCHALK

- THE BIKERS CODE -

WE KNOW THE RISK

WHEN WE RIDE

SO STOP TELLING US!!

MOTORCYCLIST

/noun (moh-ter-sy-klist)

...a person willing to take a container of flammable liquid, place it on top of a hot engine and then put the whole thing between their legs.

SCOTT D. GOTTSCHALK

IMAGINE LIFE WITHOUT MOTORCYCLES

NOW SLAP YOURSELF AND NEVER DO IT AGAIN!

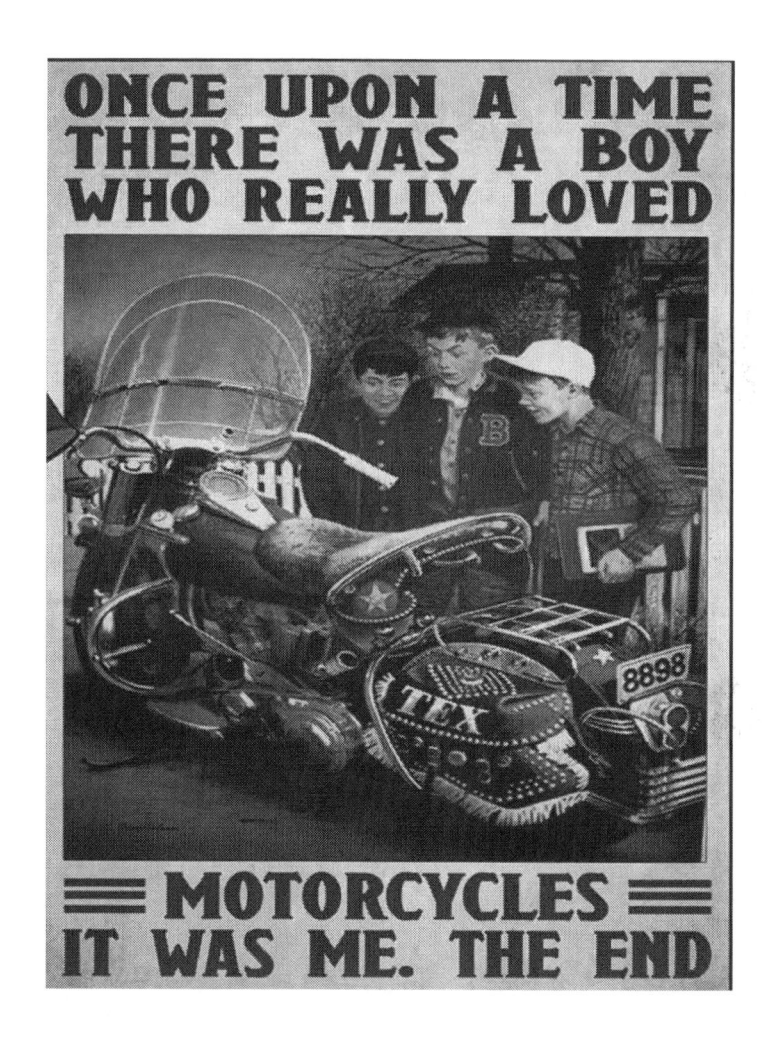

ONCE UPON A TIME THERE WAS A BOY WHO REALLY LOVED MOTORCYCLES IT WAS ME. THE END

SCOTT D. GOTTSCHALK

> **MAY I LIVE MY LIFE, THAT WHEN DEATH COMES FOR ME, EVEN HE IS SAD.**

NO BOUNDARIES TOUR

> Enjoy life so when death comes it can only take your body.

SCOTT D. GOTTSCHALK

The motorcycle is a simple solution to some of the world's most complicated problems.

NO BOUNDARIES TOUR

Everything will kill you

so choose something fun

SCOTT D. GOTTSCHALK

NO BOUNDARIES TOUR

LIFE IS NOT ABOUT
WAITING FOR THE
STORMS TO PASS
ITS ABOUT
LEARNING TO RIDE
IN THE RAIN

FRIENDS: Are for a while.
BIKER FRIENDS: Are for life

NO BOUNDARIES TOUR

SCOTT D. GOTTSCHALK

I wasnt born on a motorcycle

but I got there quick as I could!

NO BOUNDARIES TOUR

> The difference between
> Ordinary
> and
> Extraordinary
> Is that little extra

Made in the USA
Middletown, DE
17 February 2025

71007230R00157